STOP OVERTHINKING START LIVING

Eliminate negative thoughts and control your life

Simone Keys

Copyright 2023 All rights reserved©.

It is strictly forbidden to reproduce, duplicate or transmit this book's contents without the author's express written permission. In no event shall the publisher be held legally liable for any compensation, damage or monetary loss caused by the information contained in this book, either directly or indirectly.

Legal Notice:

No modification, distribution, sale, use or quotation of the contents of this book is permitted without the author's express consent.

Disclaimer Notice:

The information contained in this book is for educational and entertainment purposes only. No express or implied warranties of any kind are made. Readers acknowledge that the author is not offering legal, financial, medical or professional advice.

Index

Introduction. A path to mental liberation	7
Chapter 1. Overthinking	11
What is and what is not excessive thinking?	13
How does overthinking affect us?	15
Importance of reducing excessive thoughts	18
Overthinking: How to overcome it?	20
Chapter 2. Breaking the cycle	29
Freeing ourselves from overthinking	30
Identifying excessive thoughts	33
Coping with excessive thoughts	36
Breaking obsessive thought patterns	37
Chapter 3. Tools for mental serenity	41
Liberation through words	51
Exercise and mental balance	55
Chapter 4. Strategies for a balanced life	59

Implementing strategies	61
Designing a customized path	70
Commitment to positive mental change	75
Chapter 5. Walking to Wellness and Wholeness	79
The journey to a calmer mind	81
The power of the present	83
Chapter 6. Overthinking and its Impact	91
Excessive thoughts and stress	93
When to seek professional help?	101
Conclusion	105
Bonus 1	109
Bonus 2	113
Bonus 3	119
Bonus 4	123

Introduction

A path to mental liberation: Discover how to take control of your thoughts.

Overthinking can manifest itself in different ways in our lives: constant worrying, persistent rumination on a particular subject or obsessive thoughts, to mention just a few examples.

These psychological patterns can generate stress, anxiety and depression, limiting our ability to enjoy life and carry out our daily activities to the fullest.

Therefore, it is essential to acquire the necessary skills to help us control our thoughts and reduce their insistent rhythm.

What we think directly impacts our actions and decisions, so controlling them is vitally important.

If we allow our thoughts to become persistent and obsessive ideas about our problems, it is likely that our actions and decisions will also be negatively affected.

It has been proven that excessive thinking is associated with a higher probability of developing mental problems, such as anxiety and depression. Therefore, we will have greater physical and mental well-being by learning to manage our thoughts.

In this book, I am going to give you several strategies that can help you prevent and control excessive thoughts, and that will also help you promote your physical and mental well-being.

We will discuss meditation and mindfulness, mindful distractions, reframing negative thoughts, liberating writing and the importance of exercise, you are sure to discover powerful tools to free your mind.

Regarding meditation and mindfulness techniques, I can tell you that they are very effective in reducing the frequency and rhythm of excessive thinking.

On the one hand, meditation invites us to focus our attention on the present, leaving aside distracting or irrelevant thoughts.

On the other hand, mindfulness allows us to be aware of our thoughts, feelings and sensations without judging them.

Both methods are similar in that they allow us to regain control of our mind, of our behavior, and with this, they help us to free ourselves from recurring thoughts.

Another valuable strategy you will learn is mindful distraction, which allows you to intentionally divert your attention to activities that allow you to move away from negative thoughts and enjoy your life healthily and fully.

You will see that with simple actions such as exercising, tidying the house, reading a book, going to the movies or sharing moments with friends and family; we can enhance our ability to enjoy everything around us and thus significantly reduce the time we spend thinking in excess.

On the other hand, we will also learn to reformulate our negative thoughts, always looking for a much more optimistic perspective.

By analyzing our thoughts and finding a more positive outlook on things, we can change our attitude towards challenges and increase our chances of successfully overcoming them.

With this change of perspective, you will significantly reduce the time you spend on excessive thinking and with it, you will also strengthen your ability to deal with difficult situations that come your way.

Likewise, I also want to teach you the power of writing down your thoughts as a method of freeing your mind; you will see that by writing down your ideas in a diary or on paper and letting them go, you will advance a very important step in the process of your mental liberation.

By observing those unpleasant ideas that burden you so much from another perspective and focusing our attention on the present, you will let go of them and finally feel free of so much internal dialogue.

Last but not least, I would like to emphasize the fundamental role of regular exercise in the prevention of overthinking.

Numerous studies have confirmed the reduction of stress, anxiety and depression symptoms through regular physical exercise.

This is because physical activity releases endorphins, which are the hormones that help relieve stress and anxiety, but in addition, practicing a sporting discipline or exercising with a certain frequency will divert our attention from unfavorable thoughts and increase our ability to enjoy life in general.

It is important to remember that negative thoughts and fears are part of our human experience, but when they become persistent and hinder our lives, they need to be addressed.

In this book, I will give you the tools you need to take control of your thoughts and improve your physical and emotional well-being. However, if you do not perceive progress in your situation, it is advisable to seek the help of a professional to guide you through the process by means of a personalized plan according to your needs.

CHAPTER 1

Overthinking

Excessive thinking can become a labyrinth in our mind, a tangle of worries and reflections that takes us away from the present and prevents us from fully enjoying life.

What are excessive thoughts and how do they affect us? Here I will give you many key techniques and tools to free yourself from them and find your balance and peace of mind.

As we move forward in this journey, it is important to distinguish what is and what is not excessive thinking, so we can determine that when certain thoughts are constant in our mind, interfere with our daily activities, increase stress and anxiety, it is time to take measures to avoid and control them.

It is important to differentiate excessive thinking from healthy reflection. Occasionally, we all reflect on the past and the future, learning from our experiences and planning our actions, but the key is to recognize when thinking is obsessive, gets out of proportion and prevents us from moving forward.

The impact of overthinking encompasses different aspects of our lives: It does not allow us to live in the present, it distracts us from our responsibilities, we suffer from stress or anxiety and we become highly self-critical, and if we do not take action in time, emotional exhaustion and insecurity will be our permanent companions for an indefinite period of time.

We cannot underestimate the power of repetitive thoughts. Numerous studies have shown that their excess is linked to mental health problems such as anxiety and depression.

If our goal is to live a full life and act positively, it is very important that we know how to manage our thoughts and free ourselves from their chains.

Taking control of our thoughts requires dedication and effort, but it is not an impossible task. The first key is to become aware of the inadequate thought patterns we have adopted.

Keeping a record of our thoughts and worries in a journal can be a useful tool, particularly in identifying what our recurring patterns are, what triggers them and understanding how they tend to arise.

Once we have identified the patterns, we can begin to modify them, and cognitive reframing is a powerful ally in this task. This consists of finding alternatives and constructive approaches to counteract negative thoughts.

It is a gradual process, in which, little by little, we will realize that we are capable of facing challenges and finding solutions.

The art of mastering our thoughts does not happen overnight, it requires perseverance and constant practice, just like any other worthy goal in life. But if we commit ourselves to face our thought patterns, to recognize them and modify them, we will be very close to a fuller and more balanced life.

So, are you ready to take control of your mind?

Be aware of your thoughts, identify recurring patterns and work on modifying them. This change requires time and effort, but with it, you will be able to free yourself from excessive thinking and you will be creating a more positive and satisfying reality.

What is and what is not excessive thinking?

Overthinking is like a permanent echo in our mind, either by constantly reliving past situations or worrying excessively about the future. It focuses on the negative aspects and is usually irrational, magnifying problems beyond what is necessary.

To better understand the subject, it is useful to describe a little of its characteristics. Let me explain what they are and what they consist of:

- Excessive thinking is repeated over and over again without finding a solution or reaching a clear conclusion.
- It focuses obsessively on the same thoughts and concerns, trapping us in an endless loop of past situations or future worries.
- It arises uncontrollably and involuntarily, hindering our ability to divert our attention to other matters.
- It focuses on the negative, exaggerates the magnitude of problems and feeds anxiety and fear.

- Overthinking can affect our ability to concentrate, work performance, personal relationships and overall emotional well-being.

Characteristics of non-excessive thinking:

- Occasionally reflecting on past or future situations in a constructive manner is not considered overthinking. It is natural to learn from our experiences and grow.
- Thinking about the future and making plans is a normal part of life. The difference is in the level of worry and obsession that accompanies those thoughts.
- At certain times, it is necessary to analyze and consider different scenarios to make informed decisions. However, overthinking goes beyond this, becoming an endless cycle of worry that leads nowhere.

It is crucial to recognize the difference between healthy reflection and overthinking, as the latter can have a negative impact on our mental health and overall well-being.

It traps us in a state of constant anxiety, preventing us from fully enjoying the present and diminishing our quality of life.

How does overthinking affect us?

Reflect for a moment: How does overthinking affect you? On a daily basis, how much does overthinking impact your emotional well-being?

Losing our ability to enjoy the things and people around us is one of the most detrimental effects of overthinking.

We get lost in the midst of worries and negative thoughts, losing the possibility of savoring life. They take us away from the present and from joyful and happy experiences.

Imagine that you are with your family on a walk in the park, but your mind starts to wander about the future and you are invaded by worrying thoughts, or you start to question whether you are doing things right or whether you will be able to face the challenges ahead, and there you lose yourself, you move away from the present and stop enjoying the walk.

Instead of fully delighting in the present, your thoughts trap you in a spiral of worry that prevents you from enjoying the moment and the beauty around you.

Similarly, excessive thinking can interfere and hinder our daily activities. It distracts us, prevents us from concentrating, and this lack of focus impacts our performance, frustrates and demotivates us.

Imagine now that you are at work and you must complete an important activity, but an intrusive thought takes over your mind. For example, you start to worry excessively about making a serious mistake or about the criticism you might receive.

This constant worrying distracts you, keeps you from concentrating on the task at hand, and leads you to make mistakes that you would not normally make. As a result, your performance is affected, and you feel bad about not being able to do your job effectively.

On the other hand, anxiety and stress go hand in hand with excessive thinking. Constantly worrying about what is going to happen and anticipating negative scenarios leads to overwhelming emotional overload, creating a cycle of anxiety and stress that affects both our mental and physical health.

On this occasion, imagine that you are about to go to the job interview you have been waiting for weeks, but you start to worry, and you only think intensely about the possible difficult questions you might be asked, or about not living up to the expectations.

This anxiety and stress, generated by overthinking, leads you to feel overwhelmed, you become nervous, your heart races, you find it hard to breathe well, and you are not focused on the moment of the interview.

We cannot forget the insecurity and self-criticism that accompany us when excessive thoughts appear. We criticize ourselves and doubt our own capabilities. Insecurity holds us back, limits our personal and professional growth, and prevents us from reaching our true potential.

Now imagine you are at a gathering with friends or acquaintances and while interacting with them, you start to constantly ask yourself, "Did I say something inappropriate?", "Does everyone like me?"

These negative, self-critical thoughts undermine your confidence, make you feel insecure in social interactions, and hinder your ability to enjoy the evening.

Finally, emotional exhaustion is a direct consequence of the constant flow of excessive thoughts. When these appear, we feel overwhelmed, without energy, we lose motivation to face life's challenges, and this lack of emotional rest leads us to exhaustion and depression.

Now think that you have had a hectic day loaded with responsibilities. You get home and instead of relaxing and resting, you're just worrying, having negative thoughts about your day and what you still have to do.

At the end, you are emotionally exhausted, without energy to enjoy your rest and you cannot recharge your mood to face a new day with vitality and mental clarity.

It is important to recognize how overthinking can affect us; only then can we deal with it effectively.

Remember, you have the power to regain control of your mind and find the serenity you long for.

Importance of reducing excessive thoughts

Understanding how to reduce our excessive thoughts is the first step in making a positive turnaround in our lives. What we think has a direct impact on our actions and decisions, and if we allow intrusive thoughts to dominate us, we lose all our ability to act positively.

Numerous studies have shown that excessive thinking is associated with an increased risk of developing mental health problems such as anxiety and depression. Therefore, it is essential for our well-being to take control of our minds.

This is quite a challenge, but it is achievable with perseverance and constant effort, which requires a continuous awareness of our thoughts and a personal commitment to change destructive thought patterns.

It is not about avoiding or dismissing negative thoughts, but about adopting a different perspective and finding more optimistic ways of dealing with situations.

To master our internal dialogue, we must be aware of the thought patterns we adopt. A useful practice is to keep a record of our thoughts and concerns in a notebook or on paper.

This will help us recognize recurring patterns and themes that arise in our thoughts, and give us a deeper understanding of how they influence our daily lives.

Once we identify recurring thought patterns, we can begin to modify them. One effective technique is cognitive reframing, which involves finding an alternative perspective or constructive approach to negative thoughts.

For example, instead of thinking, "I'll never get through this," we can reframe it as "although this is a challenge right now, I have the ability to overcome it with some time and the right help." This shift in perspective helps us find solutions and develop a more positive mindset.

On the other hand, meditation and mindfulness can also help us reduce overthinking, both of which allow us to focus on the present and allow us to let go of irrelevant thoughts.

With these tools, we learn to cultivate inner calm and live in the present, and they free us from the mental burden of overthinking.

Mastering our thoughts is not something we can achieve immediately; it requires practice and determination.

Confronting our thought patterns, recognizing them and modifying them is an ongoing process that requires perseverance.

So, if you want to take control of your mind, you must cultivate awareness of your thought patterns, recognize recurring themes and strive to modify them.

Overthinking: How to overcome it?

Have you ever felt trapped in an endless cycle of thoughts? That tendency to go over and over past worries, imagine future scenarios and magnify present difficulties is bound to sound familiar.

Excessive thinking, or rumination, is exhausting and disturbing. It prevents us from fully enjoying life, makes it difficult to perform our daily tasks, and can generate negative emotions such as anxiety, sadness and stress. Don't be discouraged! I will help you discover how to overcome this pattern and find the mental balance you long for.

Each of us has a unique way of thinking and processing life events. Therefore, the perception of overthinking can vary from person to person. However, there are common symptoms that can alert us that we are falling into this detrimental cycle.

Not being able to take our mind off a difficulty, constantly aggravating and ruminating on a problem, or having trouble concentrating are symptoms that hinder our ability to enjoy life and perform our daily activities.

This is why it is essential to recognize that it is we ourselves who allow our minds to take control in this way, but why do we do it?

There are several explanations for this: Traumatic events, a stressful environment, or a complicated situation, even conflicting interpersonal relationships can generate a cycle of excessive thoughts.

Once we understand the causes of overthinking, we can take steps to overcome it. Remember that this does not happen overnight, but with practice and determination, you will be able to reduce its impact on your life.

Here are some useful strategies to control your excessive thoughts:

Awareness

The key to freeing ourselves from excessive thinking lies in the awareness of our mental processes. It is essential to be attentive to those moments in which our minds are become a whirlwind of uncontrolled thoughts, and recognize when to put a stop to them.

Being aware of our excessive thoughts implies taking control of our minds and preventing it from becoming an obstacle to our well-being.

Let us not allow our thoughts to entangle and exhaust us mentally. Let us be the guardians of our own consciousness.

When we become aware that we are experiencing excessive thinking, we move toward our liberation. We realize that we are not slaves to our thoughts and that we can stop the cycle.

It is like opening our eyes to a reality that we have unwittingly hidden for a long time. Awareness gives us the clarity we need to recognize when it is time to put an end to endless and exhausting overthinking.

Do not underestimate the power of conscience, it allows us to take control and say "no more" when excessive thoughts want to dominate us. Consciousness is basically an act of self-determination and empowerment.

So, from now on, let's be aware of our thoughts. Observe how they arise and how they happen. Recognize when they are taking up too much space in your mind and stop them. Remember that you are the master of your thoughts and that you have the power to free yourself from their captivity.

Change of perspective

Excessive thoughts can exert a stranglehold on our lives, but we have the power to challenge that control. Don't let these thoughts rule you, strive to change them and adopt a more positive outlook on reality.

The change of perspective is a powerful tool that allows us to shed negative thoughts and change them to a more optimistic and realistic approach. Sometimes, our thoughts can get stuck in an endless cycle of worries and negative assumptions; at these times, let's remember that we have the power to break that cycle.

When you find yourself trapped in excessive and dark thoughts, it's time to take control. Try with courage and determination. Change your outlook and look for the positive side of every situation.

This does not mean that you will deny the difficulties or minimize the challenges, but rather, it is about finding a balanced perspective that allows you to see the opportunities and growth potential behind every experience.

Challenge your negative thoughts and look for evidence to support a more realistic and constructive view. Your thoughts are not always an accurate representation of reality, and you have the ability to influence them.

Ask yourself: What evidence do I have to support these negative thoughts? Are there other ways of looking at this situation?

As you move into the perspective shift, don't forget the importance of being self-compassionate. Be kind to yourself when confronted with your excessive thoughts. Recognize that changing the way you think takes time and effort; it is normal to have ups and downs during this process.

You can change your thoughts and control your life. Don't let excessive thoughts define or limit you.

Focus on cultivating an optimistic and realistic outlook, which allows you to face challenges with confidence and overcome them successfully.

Distraction

At times, we find ourselves struggling to concentrate, caught in the middle of a series of excessive thoughts. However, there is an effective method to break that cycle and regain our longed-for mental clarity: conscious distraction.

Mindful distraction is a technique that allows you to take a break from your excessive thoughts, giving you a valuable mental break.

When you feel that you are scattered and find it difficult to focus on an activity, or to free yourself from overwhelming thoughts, it is time to practice distraction.

With distraction, you are not going to escape challenges or evade responsibilities; what you are going to do is to redirect your attention to activities that bring you joy and satisfaction.

A powerful way to distract yourself is reading. Choose a book that you are passionate about that transports you to other worlds and allows you to forget your worries, at least temporarily.

Through reading, you explore new ideas, emotions and perspectives, in which you can find renewed inspiration.

Music can also be a powerful ally when seeking a conscious distraction. Listen to your favorite songs, those that fill you with positive energy or invite you to dream. Let the rhythms and melodies of your favorite music transport you to a state of well-being.

Practicing an exercise is another valuable resource to divert your attention from excessive thoughts to a state of balance and peace of mind. Find a physical activity that is enjoyable and stimulating, such as running outdoors, practicing yoga or participating in group classes, something you enjoy and like to do.

You will release endorphins through movement, connect with your body, clear your mind, and gain mental clarity.

By diverting your attention to rewarding activities, you will achieve a balance that will allow you to return to your responsibilities with a much more positive outlook.

Allow yourself moments of rest and enjoy because by taking care of your mental well-being, you also strengthen your ability to face challenges more effectively.

So the next time you find it hard to concentrate, remember the importance of mindful distraction. Immerse yourself in reading, let the music envelop you or activate your body through exercise. Discover the power of diverting your attention to activities that nourish you and fill you with positive energy.

Mindfulness

Day by day, in our busy daily lives, it is easy to get caught in an endless cycle of thoughts and worries that prevent us from fully enjoying the present. However, there is a powerful tool that allows us to break this pattern and find greater mental balance: *mindfulness*.

Mindfulness invites us to consciously direct our attention to the here and now, freeing us from the burden of obsessive thoughts about the past or the future.

By practicing mindfulness, we acquire the ability to observe our thoughts and emotions without judging them or becoming attached to them; we simply let them flow.

An effective way to practice mindfulness is through meditation, dedicating a few minutes a day, sitting in a quiet place, closing our eyes and focusing our attention on our breathing.

At that moment, feel the air flow in and out of your body, allow your mind to calm down and focus on the present. With each inhalation and exhalation, gently release the thoughts that arise and return to the present.

Mindfulness is not only limited to meditation; we can incorporate it into our daily life while performing everyday tasks.

For example, when washing dishes, concentrate on each movement, the feel of the water and the sounds generated. When eating, feel the texture, color, aroma and taste of food, consciously enjoy each bite. When walking, observe your surroundings, feel the connection with the ground and become aware of each step you take.

Mindfulness helps us to detach from obsessive thoughts and find greater emotional balance. By focusing on the present and our surroundings, we begin to perceive the world more clearly and consciously. We free ourselves from worries and open ourselves to experience the fullness of each moment.

This is a practice that requires patience and consistency. Over time, you will notice how your ability to be present will strengthen and how your worries will become less overwhelming. Experience mindfulness of the present and give yourself peace and calm.

Therapy and skills acquisition

Facing excessive thoughts related to traumatic events or complicated situations can be overwhelming. However, there is a combined avenue of support that can allow you to become more mentally balanced: therapy and skill building.

Therapy gives you a safe and confidential space to explore your thoughts, emotions and experiences. With the support of a professional, you can identify and understand the cognitive patterns that fuel your excessive thoughts. It can help you discover new perspectives, inner resources and practical tools to manage the challenges you face in a healthier way.

One of the main strengths of the therapy is its personalized approach; the therapist will work with you individually, adapting techniques and approaches to your specific needs.

If your excessive thoughts are related to traumatic events, therapy can focus on emotional healing and resolution of the trauma. The therapist can help you develop effective coping strategies and build resilience if you are dealing with complicated situations.

In addition to therapy, skill acquisition is another key aspect of the transformation process. Through the development of new skills, you will expand your repertoire of tools for dealing with excessive thoughts.

These skills may include stress management techniques, effective communication, setting healthy boundaries and improving self-esteem. By acquiring them, you will end up better able to address everyday challenges and reduce the influence of excessive thoughts in your life.

The path to wellness is not linear, and each person progresses at his or her own pace. Therapy and the acquisition of skills require time, dedication and commitment. As you engage in this process, you will experience changes in the way you think, feel and act.

Don't be afraid to seek professional support and explore new avenues of personal development. Therapy and skill building will provide you with powerful tools to address your excessive thoughts and find greater emotional balance.

Let these growth opportunities guide you to a fuller and more satisfying life!

Each of us is unique, so it is important to find the approach that best suits you and your current situation.

CHAPTER 2

Breaking the cycle

It's overwhelming when incessant thoughts take over our mind, I've lived it, but I want to give you hope; you have the power to break that cycle and find the peace of mind you so desire!

The first step to freeing yourself from the cycle of overthinking is to become aware that you are caught in it and recognize the pattern. Observe your thoughts and recognize when you fall into constant ruminating and worrying. In doing so, you will distance yourself from those thoughts and begin to gain control over them.

Once you identify your overthinking patterns, it's time to challenge their veracity. Ask yourself if those thoughts are really helpful or if they distort reality. Our thoughts do not always reflect absolute truth, and we may give them less weight than we give them.

Then, practice *mindfulness* focus, pay full attention to the present without judgment or getting caught up in recurring thoughts. When you find yourself caught in a loop of thoughts, direct your attention to the present moment, focusing on your senses or your breathing.

Set mental boundaries, don't allow your thoughts to control your mind. Set restrictions, mental barriers and learn to say "no more" when they become overwhelming. Disconnect from those thoughts and focus on activities that bring you joy and peace of mind.

Seek support from friends, family or mental health professionals who can guide and support you. Sharing your concerns with people you trust will ease your mental burden and offer new perspectives.

Breaking the cycle of overthinking takes time and practice, so don't get discouraged if you encounter obstacles along the way.

Every small action you take to free your mind from these types of thoughts is a valuable accomplishment. Trust in yourself and your ability to find inner peace.

Freeing ourselves from overthinking

On our way to a calmer and more serene mind, I want to share with you several effective techniques that will undoubtedly help us to break the cycle of excessive thinking and find that longed-for inner calm.

A fundamental key to freeing ourselves from overthinking is to recognize the power of the present, to learn to live in the now. Instead of worrying about the past or worrying about the future, focus on the here and now.

Let us cultivate the ability to enjoy each moment and be aware of the wonders that surround us. In doing so, we will succeed in disengaging from negative thought patterns and create space for serenity and joy.

Mindfulness is a powerful tool for this purpose. By practicing it, we become more aware of our thoughts without allowing them to drag us down.

We observe the thoughts that arise, but we do not engage or judge them. This practice allows us to free ourselves from the control of excessive thinking and experience greater mental clarity and tranquility.

Transforming our thought patterns is another important aspect. Our thoughts can become ingrained habits.

Identifying negative thought patterns and replacing them with more positive and constructive thoughts is critical.

As we become aware of our recurring thoughts, we can question their validity and seek alternative perspectives.

Let us cultivate thoughts of gratitude, self-acceptance and confidence in our abilities. In this way, we create a new mindset that propels us toward growth and happiness.

Setting limits on our thoughts is also essential. Excessive thoughts often invade all areas of our lives. It is important to set healthy boundaries and remember that we are in control.

Let us learn to say "no" to thoughts that do not serve us and direct our attention to those that nurture and strengthen us. We create a sacred space for our inner peace and well-being by setting these boundaries.

Overthinking can drain us mentally and emotionally. To break free from this cycle, we must prioritize our self-care.

Let us take time to rest, relax and engage in activities that bring us joy and rejuvenation.

Regular exercise, a healthy diet and adequate sleep are fundamental pillars to strengthen our mind and body. Taking care of ourselves allows us to face challenges with greater resilience and mental clarity.

You are not alone on this path to freedom from overthinking. Seeking support and guidance from people close to you or mental health professionals can make a big difference.

Sharing your experiences and concerns with others can provide you with new perspectives and additional tools to overcome challenges. Together, we can support each other on this journey of growth and transformation.

Freeing ourselves from overthinking is a gradual process that requires commitment and patience. Allow yourself to take small steps each day toward a calmer and more conscious mind.

Trust in your ability to overcome obstacles and cultivate the inner peace you deserve. I am here to accompany you on this journey towards liberation from overthinking.

Identifying excessive thoughts

Both our external and internal activities have a significant impact on our minds and how we think. Spending long hours in front of a screen, being exposed to negative news or facing stressful situations can contribute to the development of excessive thinking patterns.

When we talk about "overthinking", we refer to that tendency to go over and over problems or concerns without reaching a resolution. This repetitive thinking can be detrimental to our mental and physical health, as it plunges us into an endless cycle of worry and stress.

Overthinking factors or triggers are situations, events or stimuli that trigger a negative emotional response in us. These factors can vary from person to person, but some common examples include work stress, interpersonal disputes, personal or financial difficulties, among others.

Identifying these triggers is essential to understand what causes our excessive thinking and, from there, to take effective measures to address it. If we do not avoid or properly manage excessive thoughts, a number of negative consequences can arise.

First, our mental health is affected, leading to anxiety, chronic stress and depression. In addition, these thoughts can have an impact on our physical health, weakening our immune system and increasing the risk of disease.

They can also interfere with our interpersonal relationships, as they lead us to overanalyze situations and prevent us from enjoying the present. Therefore, it is crucial to take measures to avoid excessive thinking and its consequences.

This involves developing self-regulation and stress management techniques, such as practicing mindfulness, establishing healthy boundaries in our daily activities, seeking therapeutic support, adopting relaxation habits and having a more positive and realistic approach to our thoughts.

Identifying excessive thoughts and understanding how our daily activities can influence our minds are fundamental steps to avoid falling into excessive thinking.

Here are some strategies you can use to recognize and distinguish excessive thoughts.

Pay attention to your internal dialogue: Observe your thoughts and how they play out in your mind. If you notice that you tend to circle around an issue or concern without finding a solution, you may be experiencing excessive thoughts.

Detect recurring patterns: Notice if there are themes or specifics that recur frequently in your mind. These patterns may indicate excessive thoughts. Identifying them will allow you to take steps to address them.

Examine your emotional reactions: Excessive thoughts are often accompanied by intense emotions, such as anxiety, worry or irritability. If you notice that your emotions are triggered by certain thoughts, it is likely that you are dealing with a pattern of overthinking.

Evaluate the usefulness of your thoughts: Question the usefulness and veracity of your thoughts. Ask yourself if your thoughts are based on hard facts or if they are simply your unfounded positions or concerns. This will help you discern which thoughts are excessive and will bring you no real benefit.

Observe the effects on your well-being: Reflect on how excessive thoughts affect your overall well-being. If you notice that they generate stress, anxiety or prevent you from enjoying the present, it is important to recognize them as excessive thoughts and look for ways to manage them.

Practice self-reflection: Take time to examine your thoughts and reflect on their impact on your life. Keep a journal where you record your recurring thoughts and how they make you feel. This practice will help you become aware of excessive thoughts and work on changing them.

Remember that everyone may experience excessive thoughts differently, so it is important that you find the strategies that work best for you.

Identifying excessive thoughts is the first step in dealing with them and freeing yourself from their influence on your mental well-being.

Coping with excessive thoughts

When we effectively deal with excessive thoughts, we open the door to multiple benefits for our mind and body.

Have you ever wondered, what do we gain by challenging those nagging thoughts? Let me share with you some of the most salient benefits.

By confronting excessive thoughts, we regain control over our minds and decrease the anxiety that accompanies them. By questioning and deactivating the constant cycle of worry, we can alleviate stress levels and find greater inner calm.

We gain greater mental clarity and objectivity when we recognize and label excessive thoughts. This allows us to detach emotionally from those thoughts and view them from a more rational and balanced perspective. Thus, we free ourselves from their influence and make more informed decisions.

By confronting excessive thoughts, we free ourselves from mental paralysis and are able to make decisions more effectively. By questioning the validity of those thoughts and looking for contradictory evidence, we move away from irrational worry and make decisions based on reality.

Facing excessive thoughts helps us to free ourselves from the emotional burden we carry. By practicing mindfulness and learning to let thoughts pass without holding on to them, we experience a greater sense of calm and emotional well-being. We free ourselves from the spiral of negativity and find inner peace.

We free up time and energy to focus on activities that bring us satisfaction and joy. By distracting our minds and occupying ourselves with positive activities, we improve our quality of life and find a healthier balance.

Freeing ourselves from excessive thoughts takes time, practice and patience. It is not a matter of solving everything from one day to the next. However, with perseverance and the application of the right strategies, we can experience a significant reduction in the influence of excessive thoughts in our daily lives.

Breaking obsessive thought patterns

Discovering how to break obsessive thought patterns and manage anxiety can be really beneficial to our mental health. Let me share with you an effective strategy: mindful distractions.

It is about directing our attention towards activities that are not related to those anxious and unproductive thoughts that overwhelm us.

There are a variety of ways to apply mindful distractions. Some people find engaging in useful physical hobbies such as gardening, art or exercise, while others prefer more relaxing activities, such as reading a good book or enjoying time in the company of loved ones.

The key is to find something that effectively distracts us and allows us to take our minds off those unpleasant thoughts.

It is important to keep in mind that conscious distractions are not a permanent solution to problems of overthinking and anxiety. Instead, they are tools that offer us momentary relief and help us manage our thoughts and feelings in the short term. In the long term, it is critical to learn to confront our negative thoughts rather than avoid them altogether.

An effective strategy for using conscious distractions is channel switching. It consists of recognizing the moments when we catch ourselves thinking about something unfavorable or stressful, and then making a conscious decision to replace those thoughts with more positive or helpful ones.

We can choose to remember a pleasant moment or plan something exciting instead of worrying about a problem at work. The goal is not to ignore unpleasant thoughts, but to give them less importance and direct our attention to something more optimistic.

Another useful technique is the positive anchor strategy. It consists of associating a positive thought or activity with a negative thought or situation to facilitate its recall and change our emotional state.

For example, before giving a speech, we can recall a previous accomplishment or listen to a song that makes us feel secure and confident. These strategies help us change how we feel and distract our minds from the unpleasant experience.

Remember that conscious distractions should be done consciously, not as a way to escape or avoid problems. It is important to acquire the skills necessary to face challenges head on and resolve them productively.

Mindful distractions are a useful tool for controlling excessive thoughts and anxiety. They allow us to divert our attention to more constructive and positive activities, giving us temporary relief and helping us to better manage our thoughts and emotions.

However, it is essential to learn to cope with and solve problems over the long term. Conscious distractions are only one part of the personal growth process and must be used in conjunction with other strategies to achieve lasting mental well-being.

Let me accompany you on this journey to a calmer and more balanced mind.

CHAPTER 3

Tools for mental serenity

There are many valuable tools that we can use to reduce repetitive thoughts, which also contribute to improve our physical and mental well-being.

Next, I will present some of them, so that you can make the most of their benefits, some of them you can practice on your own, for others, although you can execute them yourself, it is advisable to the accompaniment of a specialist. Finally, there are others that require the guidance of a professional in the area.

Find out how these tactics can help you control overthinking and find the mental serenity you crave!

Relaxing activities

Spending time in relaxing activities is essential to reduce excessive thinking and promote mental serenity. Yoga, meditation and tai chi are examples of activities that can help you find a state of calm and balance.

By practicing these activities, it allows you to disconnect from daily worries and focus on the present moment. For example, doing a yoga session at the end of the day gives you the opportunity to stretch and relax your body while helping you to release accumulated tension and calm your mind.

This therapy is an excellent option to start reducing excessive thinking. You can do activities such as taking a relaxing bath, practicing deep breathing, listening to soft music or reading a book that inspires tranquility.

These practices can be easily done at home and give you a space to disconnect and find calm in the midst of the daily routine.

Physical activity

Regular physical exercise is a powerful tool to reduce overthinking and promote peace of mind.

When we move and exercise, we release endorphins, hormones that generate feelings of well-being and happiness. In addition, exercise allows us to disconnect from worrisome thoughts and focus on our body and movement.

For example, going for a run or a bike ride can be an effective way to release accumulated stress and improve our overall mental health.

Regular exercise is a powerful tool for improving both physical and mental well-being. You can choose an activity that you enjoy, such as walking, running or swimming. As you spend time moving your body, you will release endorphins and reduce stress, which in turn will help calm your mind.

Writing - Burning

This method consists of writing your recurring thoughts and worries on a piece of paper and then burning it to symbolically free yourself from their weight. In doing so, you are releasing your thoughts and allowing yourself to let go of what is weighing you down.

You could write all those worries on a piece of paper and then, by burning it, symbolize the act of letting go of those insecurities and allowing yourself to move forward without the burden of those limiting thoughts.

You can perform this ritual in the privacy of your home, creating a quiet and safe space for yourself. It is a symbolic way to let go of what disturbs you and open space for new positive thoughts and emotions.

Reduce news and social networking time

We are constantly exposed to negative news and comparison on social media. Both can generate anxiety and overthinking, so reducing the time we spend on social media can be a

can be an effective strategy to maintain mental serenity.

This therapy involves becoming aware of the amount of time spent consuming news and surfing social networks, and gradually reducing that time.

Set clear boundaries and specific times, daily or weekly, to review news and social media and avoid overexposure to negative or stressful information. This will allow you to have more control over the information you consume and avoid mental overload.

This practice is completely accessible and you can implement it in your day-to-day life to foster greater peace of mind.

Positive self-hypnosis

Positive self-hypnosis is a technique in which you use visualizations, suggestions and affirmations to reprogram your mind towards more positive and constructive thoughts.

You can record your own positive affirmations and listen to them periodically, especially at times when you feel overwhelmed by negative thoughts.

For example, if you find yourself constantly thinking about your physical flaws, you could record affirmations such as "I love and accept myself as I am" or "I am unique and beautiful in many ways." By repeating these affirmations, you are training your mind to focus on positive thoughts and move away from destructive self-criticism.

This therapy allows you to harness the power of your subconscious mind to change negative thought patterns and foster serenity.

Attitude of gratitude

Gratitude is a powerful tool for cultivating mental serenity. By focusing on the things you are grateful for, you shift your perspective toward the positive and away from negative rumination.

You can create the habit of writing down three things you are grateful for every day, simple things like the sun shining in the sky or the aroma of your coffee in the morning. By recognizing and appreciating the little things in life, it opens you up to a more positive and serene mindset.

In addition to keeping a gratitude journal, you can also practice acknowledging and expressing gratitude to others. This technique is accessible to do at home and can have a significant impact on your emotional well-being.

Logical thinking

This approach consists of questioning and challenging your negative and excessive thoughts from a logical perspective. For example, if you have the recurring thought, "No one respects me," you can ask yourself: Is there any evidence that this is true in all situations? Are there people who show me respect?

By challenging your thoughts and looking for contrary evidence, you may realize that your negative thoughts are not always grounded in reality.

Identify your automatic negative thoughts and look for evidence or proof to support or refute them. By applying logical thinking, you can challenge and modify your limiting thought patterns, generating greater mental serenity.

Meditation

This ancient practice helps us to cultivate mindfulness and mental calm. There are different approaches to meditation, such as mindfulness, relaxation meditation and transcendental meditation. All can be effective in reducing excessive thinking and promoting mental serenity.

Spend 10 minutes a day to sit quietly and focus on your breathing. This can have a significant impact on your mental well-being.

There are numerous guides and apps available to help you get started in meditation at home as well, although you can seek out local groups or classes to deepen your practice.

Modify lifestyle

Sometimes small changes in our lifestyle can have a big impact on our mental serenity. These changes can include setting healthy boundaries, learning to delegate tasks, establishing structured routines, or seeking moments of solitude and self-care.

For example, if you find yourself constantly exhausted from taking on too many responsibilities, you could learn to say "no" when necessary and prioritize your emotional well-being.

Evaluate aspects such as your diet, quality of sleep, time management, interpersonal relationships and self-care habits and consciously make positive adjustments that promote your mental well-being.

Conscious distraction

When negative and repetitive thoughts threaten to overwhelm you, conscious distraction can be a useful strategy, divert your attention to pleasurable or interesting activities to temporarily remove yourself from intrusive thoughts.

For example, if you find yourself caught in a spiral of anxious thoughts, you might choose to read a book, listen to music, do a craft or go for a walk.

By focusing on something different, on activities that you find interesting or pleasurable, you allow your mind to relax and find respite.

Acceptance

Acceptance is key to finding mental serenity. It is about recognizing and accepting thoughts and emotions without judging them or fighting against them. It involves learning to accept your present thoughts, emotions and circumstances without judging or resisting them, to allow them to flow without clinging to them or trying to change them.

For example, if you find yourself worrying about a problem that you cannot solve at the moment, you can say to yourself, "I accept that this thought is present, but it does not define me and I can let it go." By practicing acceptance, you can free yourself from inner struggle and find greater inner peace.

Accepting what is out of your control and focusing on what you can change will help you find greater inner peace.

Opposing thought

This strategy consists of identifying your automatic negative thoughts, challenging them, and replacing them with alternative, positive and more realistic opposite thoughts.

For example, if you find yourself thinking, "I'm not smart enough for this job," you can replace it with the opposite thought, "I have the skills and ability to learn and grow in this job."

You can counteract overthinking and improve your mental well-being by training your mind to focus on positive, constructive thoughts.

20% rule

This strategy involves reducing and limiting your responsibilities and commitments based on the principle that, in most situations, 20% of your efforts produce 80% of the results.

By setting more realistic boundaries and prioritizing your well-being, you'll have more room to take care of yourself and reduce your mental load. Instead of obsessing over perfection and exhausting yourself trying to get everything done, you can identify the most important tasks and actions and focus on them.

For example, if you have an overwhelming to-do list, you can prioritize the three tasks that will really make a difference and focus your energies on them. By simplifying and prioritizing, you can reduce the mental load and find greater balance in your life.

Although this strategy can be applied on your own, it is beneficial to have the support and guidance of a professional to implement it effectively.

CBT - Cognitive-Behavioral Therapy

It is a recognized and successful approach in psychotherapy. Its main objective is to identify and modify destructive patterns of thought and behavior. Through this therapy, you will be able to work with a therapist to recognize your negative thought patterns and replace them with more positive and realistic ones.

For example, if you have the constant thought, "I'm not good enough," you could learn to replace it with more realistic thoughts such as "I have unique skills and qualities that make me valuable. CBT gives you concrete tools to transform your thinking and find greater mental balance.

This therapy is a therapeutic approach widely used to treat mental disorders and improve emotional well-being. It focuses on identifying and changing negative thought and behavior patterns, promoting greater mental serenity.

It is most effective when done with a specialized therapist, but you can also find CBT resources and techniques that you can apply at home.

Exposure therapy

Exposure therapy is mainly used in the treatment of anxiety disorders and consists of exposing ourselves gradually and under the supervision of a therapist,

to the situations or stimuli that generate fear and trigger our anxiety. Through direct exposure to the feared stimuli, we can learn to regulate our anxiety and manage stress more effectively.

For example, if you have a fear of the outdoors, you could start by taking short walks outdoors and gradually increase the duration and distance. Over time, you will find that your fears diminish and that you can face situations that used to make you anxious.

This therapy can be performed autonomously in certain cases, but it is advisable to have professional support to design an adequate and safe exposure plan.

These valuable tools will provide you with various ways to control excessive thinking and cultivate mental serenity. You can experiment with them and adapt them to your own personal growth process.

Remember that each person is unique, so it is important to find the therapies and techniques that best suit your needs and preferences.

Whenever necessary, do not hesitate to seek the help of a specialist to receive adequate support in your process towards mental serenity.

Liberation through words

A powerful strategy for dealing with overthinking and anxiety is to put our thoughts down on paper and let them out into the world. Have you considered keeping a journal? This practice has the potential to bring us greater mental clarity and peace of mind by releasing our thoughts.

Writing down our thoughts rather than holding them in our minds offers us numerous benefits by allowing them to flow through writing.

It also allows us to organize and prioritize our ideas and concerns more effectively, allowing us to look at our thoughts from an objective and fresh perspective. This can lead us to see our concerns in a new light and obtain more useful answers.

Writing and venting our thoughts has many advantages. One of them is that it helps us to recognize negative thought patterns and gives us the opportunity to develop strategies to overcome them.

By writing down our thoughts and concerns, we are able to identify the usual recurring ones and choose the best way to address them. In addition, writing allows us to process our feelings in a more rational way, enabling us to find a clearer perspective.

It is important to keep in mind that writing down our ideas and releasing them is a technique that provides short-term benefits and is not a permanent solution to overthinking and worrying.

Therefore, it is crucial to address our difficulties effectively, learn to relax and look at events that do not normally generate stress from a calm and practical perspective. Learning to do this correctly is fundamental.

So where do we start? Start writing down your ideas, concerns and reflections in a journal or notepad in order to clear your mind and achieve greater clarity and calm.

By writing down our ideas and getting them out, we can better focus on what really matters and work toward constructive solutions. In addition, this process allows us to gain a new perspective on our thoughts, recognize destructive thought patterns and improve our ability to manage our emotions.

The act of writing down our ideas and letting them flow can increase our self-awareness. As we write down our ideas, reflections and concerns, we will better understand how our thoughts and feelings influence our daily lives and how we can manage them appropriately.

It is essential to have a safe and discreet place where we can write and express our opinions without restrictions. This will help us to see our thoughts from a new perspective, recognize harmful thought patterns, improve our ability to process our feelings, set goals and objectives, and increase our level of self-awareness.

If you have difficulty controlling your excessive thoughts and anxiety, remember that writing down your thoughts and letting them go is only a temporary tool.

However, the process of writing down and releasing your thoughts can also be a way to keep a record of how you have managed problems and thoughts over time. This record can help you observe your progress and make informed decisions about how to continue to control overthinking.

It is important to perform this exercise on an ongoing basis to identify thought patterns and tendencies, as well as to seek effective solutions.

This strategy can be useful to prevent overthinking from becoming a major problem and improve our mental and emotional health in a holistic way.

Writing down our thoughts and letting them go can be beneficial not only for people who experience anxiety or overthinking, but also for anyone who wishes to improve their mental and emotional well-being.

It is an effective tool for processing feelings and experiences, setting goals and objectives, and keeping track of the control of our thoughts and emotions throughout the process.

Practical Exercise: Writing and Letting Go
- Get a notebook and pen or pencil, or open a note-taking app on your mobile device or computer.
- Take a few moments to relax and focus on your breathing.
- Start writing without pausing or censoring yourself. Do not try to correct the text at this point. Write everything that comes to your mind.
- Keep writing until you feel you have nothing more to say.

- Read what he has written. Do you observe negative or recurring thought patterns?
- Take note of these trends on a separate page.
- Make a list of pessimistic or restrictive thoughts and, for each one, write an optimistic or reality-based response.
- Delete the note by destroying it, burning it, throwing it away, deleting it or closing the note application.
- Take a moment to reflect on the activity and how you feel about it now that you have released your thoughts.
- Repeat this exercise when you feel overwhelmed by your thoughts, you can also do it daily. By writing down what you are thinking and releasing it, you will have a clearer mind and it will relieve the possible emotional pressure you may be suffering from.

Exercise and mental balance

Physical exercise plays a fundamental role in maintaining our mental balance. By participating regularly in physical activities, we can obtain numerous benefits for our mental and emotional health.

Don't underestimate the power that movement has on our brain and our mood. When we exercise, our brain releases endorphins, those wonderful chemicals that make us feel good and reduce pain.

Endorphins act as natural painkillers, and not only that, they can also relieve stress, anxiety and depression. It's as if our body gives us a dose of happiness and tranquility every time we move.

But the benefits don't stop there. Regular exercise can improve the quality of our sleep, increase our self-esteem and give us an overall sense of satisfaction. So why not take advantage of all these benefits that exercise brings?

The choice of type of exercise depends on your personal preferences. Some people enjoy more vigorous activities such as running, swimming or team sports.

Others prefer quieter, more mindful exercises such as yoga or tai chi. No matter what your choice is, the important thing is to find an activity that you really enjoy and that motivates you to move on a regular basis.

In addition to the chemical impact on our brain, exercise can also help us balance our minds by providing us with dedicated time to ourselves.

During exercise, it is common that worries and stress are reduced as we concentrate on movement and physical sensations. It is as if our mind finds a break and can disconnect from daily stresses.

And that's not all. Physical exercise can serve as a form of healthy escape. When we find ourselves stuck in negative thoughts or a low mood, exercising can help us shift our focus and distract us from those emotions.

It is as if we were releasing all that mental load through the movement of our body. In addition, if we choose to exercise in a group, we can encourage socialization.

Connecting with others while exercising strengthens our social connections and contributes to improving our emotional well-being. Exercise becomes a shared space where we essentially support each other and find motivation.

It is advisable to establish a regular and consistent routine to get the maximum benefits of exercise on our mental balance. Find the time of day that works best for you and allows you to incorporate physical activity consistently into your life.

Remember that strenuous activity is not necessary for mental benefits. Even small doses of exercise can make a big difference.

Physical exercise is a powerful tool for maintaining our mental balance. By releasing endorphins and reducing stress, exercise can improve our mood, increase our self-esteem and promote an overall sense of well-being.

So I encourage you to incorporate exercise into your daily routine as an effective strategy to take care of both your physical health and mental well-being.

CHAPTER 4.

Strategies for a balanced life

Let us now consider a new perspective, one that will allow us to grow and develop more fully in our daily lives.

Authenticity is the key to living a full and meaningful life. Being true to yourself and living in accordance with your values and beliefs gives you a sense of integrity and satisfaction.

Know yourself and accept yourself as you are, with all your strengths and weaknesses. By embracing your authenticity, you allow yourself to blossom and shine in a unique way.

Personal growth implies being open to change and continuous learning. The world is constantly evolving, and you too must evolve to adapt and grow.

Cultivate a growth mindset where you see challenges as opportunities for learning and development. Never stop looking for new ways to expand your knowledge and skills.

Gratitude is a powerful engine of happiness and well-being. Practicing gratitude daily helps you focus on the positive and appreciate the blessings in your life.

Take time to reflect on the things you are grateful for, whether big or small. Gratitude connects you to the abundance around you and fills you with joy and satisfaction.

Resilience is an essential skill for overcoming life's challenges and adversities. Learning to adapt and recover from difficulties allows you to face obstacles with courage and determination. Cultivate resilience by developing an optimistic mindset, seeking support from others and taking care of your physical and emotional well-being.

Purpose is what gives meaning and direction to your life. Discovering your purpose helps you set clear goals and focus on what really matters.

Ask yourself what you are passionate about and how you can use your talents and skills to make a difference in the world. Find your purpose and work towards it with passion and dedication.

Connecting with others is fundamental to our emotional and social well-being. Cultivate meaningful, genuine relationships where you can be authentic and mutually supportive.

Take time to be present with your loved ones, actively listen and show empathy. Human connections nurture us and give us a sense of belonging and love.

Focus on the present and practice mindfulness in your daily life. The past has passed and the future has not yet arrived. The only real moment is now.

Learn to savor each experience, no matter how small, and be fully present in the present moment. Mindfulness helps you find inner calm and enjoy the beauty of life.

Ask yourself how you can apply these principles to your own life, and how to live in a more authentic, meaningful and fulfilling way.

You are the author of your own story. You have the power to create the life you desire and deserve. Embrace your authenticity, cultivate personal growth, practice gratitude, develop resilience, find your purpose, connect with others and live fully in the present.

Implementing strategies

Let us now try to implement some strategies in our daily routine, some methods and approaches that will help us in many ways, especially to relieve us from the tormenting coming and going of recurring thoughts.

Did you know that the key to a fuller and more meaningful life is to be present in each moment? *Mindfulness* can be a useful tool to stop thinking repetitively and achieve a calmer and more balanced mind.

Here are some simple examples from everyday life where mindfulness can help you control repetitive thoughts and find calm.

Imagine you have an important presentation at work and you are feeling overwhelmed with stress. By practicing meditation and mindfulness, you can take a moment to sit quietly, close your eyes and focus your attention on your breathing.

As you focus on your breath, you become aware of the stressful thoughts that arise in your mind. Instead of getting caught up in them, you observe them as passing clouds and gently turn your attention to the sensation of the breath. This allows you to detach from the stressful thoughts and find calm in the present moment.

Many people experience repetitive thoughts and worries before going to bed, making it difficult to fall asleep. Practicing mindfulness before bedtime can be helpful in this case.

You can spend a few minutes sitting or lying down quietly, focusing on your breathing and letting thoughts come and go without getting caught up in them.

By directing your attention to the present and allowing thoughts to flow, you can free yourself from nagging suspicions and prepare for a peaceful sleep.

Sometimes, you may find yourself in adverse social situations that trigger repetitive thoughts and anxiety. Mindfulness can help you manage these situations.

Before entering a social event or meeting, you can take a moment to focus on your breathing and tune into your physical sensations.

As you interact with others, practice listening fully, paying full attention to what they are saying and how you are feeling at that moment.

If repetitive or critical thoughts about yourself arise, simply observe them without judgment and redirect your attention to the present moment and the ongoing interaction.

These are just a few examples of how meditation and mindfulness can help you control repetitive thoughts and cultivate mental calmness in everyday situations.

By regularly practicing meditation and mindfulness, you will strengthen your ability to observe your thoughts without being carried away by them, which will allow you to have a calmer and more balanced mind in your daily life.

Sometimes, negative or stressful thoughts can overwhelm us. But here comes an interesting strategy: conscious distraction! Instead of fighting those thoughts, you can consciously choose to distract yourself from them.

Mindful Distraction, also known as mindful attention shifting, is a technique you can use to interrupt repetitive thought patterns and redirect your attention to something more present and calm.

Instead of trying to suppress or directly stop repetitive thoughts, Conscious Distraction invites you to consciously shift your focus to something more neutral or positive.

Conscious Distraction provides you with an effective strategy to interrupt repetitive thoughts and find mental calm.

By practicing it on a regular basis, you can train your mind to consciously shift its focus and free yourself from negative or troubling mental patterns that trap you.

For example, when you find yourself caught in a spiral of worry, you can choose to read an inspirational book, listen to your favorite music, or take a walk in nature. These activities will help you divert your attention to something positive and comforting.

Here are some other simple examples from everyday life where Conscious Distraction can help you control repetitive thoughts and achieve greater mental calm.

When you find yourself caught in a cycle of repetitive thoughts, you can practice mindful distraction by focusing on your breathing. Take a moment to breathe deeply and pay attention to the physical sensations of inhaling and exhaling.

With each conscious breath, you shift from repetitive thoughts to the present experience of your breath, which can help calm your mind.

Another way to consciously distract yourself from repetitive thoughts is to focus on your senses. You can choose a specific sense, such as sight or hearing, and pay attention to what you see or hear in the immediate environment.

Observe colors, shapes, sounds or any other detail that captures your attention. By directing your focus to the sensory stimuli present, you decrease attention to recurring thoughts.

When you find yourself caught in repetitive negative or worrisome thoughts, you can practice mindful distraction by cultivating gratitude.

Take a moment to reflect on the things you are grateful for in your life. You can list the positive things you have mentally or in writing, such as relationships, accomplishments, or rewarding experiences.

By shifting your attention to gratitude, you shift the energy of your thoughts and create a sense of calm and appreciation.

Engaging in mindful physical activity, such as taking a walk, stretching or practicing yoga, can help you distract yourself from repetitive thoughts and connect with your body.

As you engage in the activity, pay attention to physical sensations, movement and breathing. This will help you shift your attention to the present and away from recurring thought patterns.

Let's talk about another technique that can help us silence repetitive thoughts: Positive anchoring. Did you know that you can associate positive feelings with specific objects or activities?

For example, if you want to remember feelings of joy, you can choose to listen to a happy song that makes you smile, or if you are looking for serenity, you can create a corner in your home with relaxing elements such as scented candles or a plant.

These positive anchors consist of consciously associating a stimulus or an experience with positive emotions or calming mental states, that is, they act as memories of positive emotions and help you recover your emotional balance in times of stress.

Viewed in this way, positive anchors can be seen as effective tools for interrupting repetitive thought patterns and fostering a calmer, more positive mindset.

By practicing mindfulness with positive anchors, you can redirect your attention to them and cultivate greater mental calm.

Here are some simple examples from everyday life where positive anchors can help you control repetitive thoughts and have a calm mind:

If you find yourself stuck in a cycle of repetitive thoughts, you can create a positive anchor by associating a relaxing song or melody with a sense of calm. You can take a moment to close your eyes, breathe deeply and listen to the music with mindfulness.

With time and practice, when faced with repetitive thoughts, you can remember the soothing music and use it as an anchor to bring calm to your mind.

Nature can be a powerful positive anchor for calming the mind. If you find yourself stuck in repetitive thoughts, you can practice mindfulness by getting outdoors and connecting with nature.

Observe the trees, plants, colors and textures around you. Become aware of physical sensations, such as the breeze on your skin or the sound of birds. In doing so, allow the beauty and serenity of nature to become a positive anchor to divert your attention from repetitive thoughts.

Another way to use positive anchors is to recall happy moments or experiences in your life. You can bring to mind a specific memory in which you felt happy, fulfilled or at peace.

Focus on the details of that memory and immerse yourself in the associated positive emotions. By remembering and reliving these positive experiences, you can consciously change your state of mind and move away from repetitive thoughts.

Cultivating gratitude is another positive anchor you can use to calm the mind. You can practice mindfulness by taking a moment to list mentally or in writing the things you are grateful for in your life.

By focusing on the blessings and positive things you have, you shift your perspective and shift your attention to more positive and calm states of mind.

By practicing mindfulness with positive anchors, you can interrupt repetitive thought patterns and find calm in your daily life.

Remember that the key is regular, conscious practice to strengthen your positive anchors and allow them to guide you to a calmer, more balanced mind.

A last but not least technique for silencing repetitive thoughts is exposure treatment, a technique used in cognitive-behavioral therapy to confront and reduce the intensity of repetitive or intrusive thoughts.

Sometimes, facing your fears gradually can help you overcome them. Instead of avoiding or suppressing intrusive thoughts, a gradual and controlled exposure to them will diminish their power and you will learn to deal with them more effectively.

For example, if you have a fear of public speaking, you can start by practicing in front of a mirror, then with a close friend, and finally in a more challenging environment.

This technique allows you to gradually desensitize yourself and gain self-confidence. Remember, taking small courageous steps can make big strides in your personal growth.

Mindfulness can be a complementary tool in this process by helping you remain calm and accepting while dealing with recurring thoughts.

Imagine that you have a repetitive thought related to safety, this thought invades you and causes you anxiety, such as the constant worry that something bad might happen to a loved one. To address this, you could implement a gradual, controlled exercise.

Become aware of repetitive thinking. Recognize and label the intrusive thought when it pops into your mind. For example, you can tell yourself the thought, "There's that safety concern again."

Practice mindfulness. Instead of getting caught up in the content of the thought or fighting against it, use mindfulness to observe it without judgment.

Sit in a quiet place, focus on your breathing and observe how the thought appears and disappears in your mind, like a cloud floating in the sky.

Gradual exposure. Once you feel comfortable practicing mindfulness with the repetitive thought present, you can move to the next stage, which involves consciously exposing yourself to the content of the thought.

For example, you can visualize a specific situation that causes you concern, such as your loved one facing potential danger.

Maintain mindfulness during the thought: As you gradually expose yourself to the exposure, keep your mindfulness in the present moment. Observe your emotional and physical reactions without judgment.

As you practice mindfulness during exposure, you will begin to notice that the intensity of the repetitive thought decreases over time.

It is important to note that exposure treatment is most effective when guided by a trained mental health professional.

If you experience repetitive or intrusive thoughts that negatively diminish your well-being, I recommend you seek the support of a therapist to receive a proper evaluation and personalized treatment.

All of these strategies are simple, yet powerful. I invite you to integrate them into your daily life and experience the positive changes they can generate.

Remember, the path to a full and satisfying life begins with small, conscious actions.

Designing a customized path

Facing recurring thoughts can be exhausting and frustrating, but there is a way to regain control and calm the mind.

Designing a personalized path tailored to your needs and preferences to calm your mind and stop wasting time with recurring thoughts will allow you to develop effective strategies to improve your emotional well-being.

This individualized approach requires that we follow a few fundamental steps to design our own path and achieve a calmer and calmer mind.

Self-awareness. The first step in addressing recurring thoughts is to recognize the patterns that are repeating in your mind.

Take some time to reflect on your recurring thought patterns and how they happen to you. Identify the issues or situations that tend to trigger those thoughts.

This will help you to better understand how your thoughts work, what triggers their repetition and to set clear goals.

If you suffer from excessive thoughts, it is important to understand and address this experience in order to maintain good mental health.

These are questions that can help you explore and better understand your excessive thoughts, but don't limit yourself to them. There are many others that you can ask yourself in order to get to know yourself better:

- How often do you experience recurring or intrusive thoughts that you cannot control?
- Do your excessive thoughts cause you anxiety, stress or emotional discomfort?
- Do you have difficulty concentrating or performing tasks because of your excessive thoughts?
- Do you feel that your excessive thoughts prevent you from enjoying the present or living in the moment?
- Are your excessive thoughts related to specific considerations, such as work, personal relationships or health?
- Have you noticed any patterns in your excessive thinking, such as always thinking the worst or constantly anticipating problems?
- Do you have repetitive rituals or behaviors that you try to perform to calm your excessive thoughts?
- Have you sought professional help, such as a therapist or psychologist, to address your excessive thoughts?
- Have you noticed any connection between your excessive thoughts and stressful situations in your life?

- What strategies have you tried so far to manage your excessive thoughts and adequate have been the results?

Set realistic goals. Define specific and achievable, realistic goals to calm your mind and reduce recurring thoughts. These goals should be specific and measurable.

For example, you can aim to meditate for 10 minutes a day or practice mindfulness during certain key moments. Setting realistic goals will help you stay motivated and help you measure your progress.

Use strategies. Identify effective strategies that will help you cope with recurring thoughts. You can try different techniques, such as meditation, mindful breathing, cognitive reframing, or therapeutic writing.

Find the strategies that work best for you and use them as tools to calm your mind in times of overthinking.

Practice mindfulness. Mindfulness is a powerful tool for calming the mind and reducing recurring thoughts.

Take time each day to practice mindfulness, either through meditation, mindful observation or simply paying full attention to your daily activities. This will help you to be present in the present moment and let go of thoughts that don't serve you.

Identify and challenge your limiting beliefs. Recurring thoughts are often linked to limiting or negative beliefs about yourself and the world.

Identify those beliefs and question their validity. Look for evidence that contradicts them and replace them with more realistic and positive thoughts.

Find activities that calm you. Find out what activities help you calm your mind and reduce recurring thoughts.

It can be walking outdoors, practicing yoga, painting, reading or any other activity that brings you peace and tranquility. Make space in your daily routine to dedicate time to these activities and prioritize them.

Set technological limits. Too much time on electronic devices can increase recurrent thoughts.

Set healthy boundaries for technology use, such as turning off devices before bedtime or assigning specific times of the day to check your messages or social media. This will help you free your mind from distractions and find greater balance.

Don't try to handle it all by yourself: Remember that you don't have to deal with recurring thoughts by yourself. Seek support from family, friends or mental health professionals.

If you feel that the recurring thoughts are significantly improving your emotional well-being and quality of life, consider seeking professional support.

A therapist or counselor can provide you with additional tools and guidance to deal with recurring thoughts effectively.

Periodically review and evaluate progress: It is important to periodically review and evaluate the progress you have made on your journey to calm your mind.

Observe how your abilities to manage recurring thoughts have improved and evaluate whether your strategies are proving effective. Making adjustments and adaptations as needed will help you maintain steady progress.

Sharing your challenges and experiences with people you trust can give you a new perspective and emotional support.

Follow a planned action plan. Following a well-structured action plan has been shown to be effective in reducing overthinking.

Developing a detailed and realistic action plan is one of the most important factors in determining success in reducing recurrent thoughts.

Designing a personalized path to calm the mind and stop wasting time with recurring thoughts requires time, patience and self-discovery.

People who have a plan are more likely to be consistent in adopting tactics to reduce overthinking.

By recognizing patterns, setting clear goals, using effective strategies and seeking support, you can achieve a calmer, calmer mind.

Remember that each person is unique, so it is important to find the strategies and techniques that work best for you.

Be kind to yourself during this process and celebrate each small step toward a calmer mind free of recurring thoughts.

Commitment to positive mental change

Let's face together the challenge of opting for a positive mental change. This commitment invites us to dedicate our thoughts to transforming negative or limiting patterns into more constructive and optimistic thoughts.

We can develop a resilient, empowered, and hopeful mindset through a proactive and conscious stance. Here are some guidelines for you to fully commit to this positive mental shift:

Self-awareness: The first step on the road to positive mental change is to become aware of our current thought patterns. Take time to observe your thoughts and how they emerge emotionally. Identify those negative or self-critical patterns that seem to repeat themselves in your mind over and over again.

Challenging Negative Thoughts: Once you have identified these negative thought patterns, it is time to challenge them. Question their veracity and validity. Ask yourself if there is real evidence to support those thoughts or if you are interpreting situations in a distorted way. Replace those negative thoughts with positive, realistic affirmations that propel you forward.

Gratitude practice: Cultivating gratitude is a powerful tool for shifting toward a more positive mindset. Take time each day to acknowledge and be grateful for the good things in your life, no matter how small. This exercise will help you shift the focus from negatives to positives and develop a more optimistic outlook overall.

Focus on self-care: Taking care of yourself, both physically and emotionally, is essential to foster positive mental change. Prioritize activities that bring you joy and well-being, such as getting regular exercise, getting adequate rest, eating healthy, and participating in activities that relax and rejuvenate you.

Learning and growth: Commit to continuous learning and growth. Seek opportunities for personal development, whether through reading, participating in courses or workshops, or learning new skills. Stimulating your mind and acquiring new knowledge will help you broaden your perspective and generate a positive change in your mindset.

Persistence and patience: Changing ingrained negative thought patterns takes time and effort. Maintain an attitude of persistence and patience with yourself. Recognize that positive mental change is a gradual process and that every small step you take counts. Celebrate your accomplishments and don't be discouraged by the setbacks you may encounter along the way.

Positive mental change requires a constant and conscious commitment. By practicing these guidelines regularly and consistently, you will experience a gradual transformation in your mindset.

You will be amazed at how your emotional well-being is strengthened and how you develop greater resilience to face life's challenges.

This commitment to positive mental change can become a beacon of hope and an engine for growth and happiness in your life.

CHAPTER 5

Walking to wellness and wholeness

Recognizing negative patterns and promoting change is the first step towards mental liberation; it is being aware of the negative patterns of thought and behavior that harm us.

But this is only the beginning of a long road composed of various alternatives, which if we are willing to walk, will give us great satisfaction and peace of mind, so let's see what aspects can be part of this road.

Cultivate mindfulness and meditation: Mindfulness and meditation are powerful practices for calming the mind and being fully present at the moment, by incorporating them into our daily routine, we can experience the benefits of a calmer, clearer mind.

Establish positive anchors: Creating positive anchors helps us to connect with positive emotions and sensations. By using these anchors, we can change our state of mind and foster greater satisfaction and well-being.

Develop an action plan with daily steps: A concrete action plan gives us the structure we need to implement positive changes in our daily lives. Designing a plan that includes activities that we enjoy, writing in a journal and regular participation in physical activities, among others, will be a great step towards our serenity and peace of mind.

Surround ourselves with optimistic and encouraging people: Our social environment influences our mental health. It is of great importance to surround ourselves with optimistic and encouraging people, as they will support us in our personal growth and help us overcome difficulties.

Maintaining healthy relationships and building a support network: Healthy relationships and a support network ensure a sense of belonging and emotional support. Maintaining healthy relationships and building a network of valuable people in our lives is critical to moving forward on our path toward calming our minds.

Seek professional help when needed: If we experience persistent symptoms of anxiety, sadness or stress, it is important to seek help from a trained expert. Recognizing when we need additional support is a valuable step toward taking care of our mental health.

Explore different approaches and techniques: Each person is unique, so it is important to try different approaches and techniques to find the ones that work best for us. There are a variety of methods, from meditation to negative thought reconstruction, and after trying them out and deciding which one works best for us, we can adapt them to our specific needs.

Cultivate patience and perseverance: The process of mental liberation requires time and dedication. Let us learn to cultivate the patience and perseverance necessary to overcome obstacles and remain committed to our personal growth.

Enjoying the journey to wellness and personal growth: Mental liberation is a personal and rewarding journey. As we immerse ourselves in our process of self-knowledge, let us remember to enjoy each step and celebrate our achievements on the path to a freer mind and greater well-being.

Mental liberation is a path that allows us to achieve a more balanced and meaningful life. By applying these strategies, we can experience a positive transformation in our mental and emotional health.

Let us remember that self-discovery and personal growth are continuous processes, and with dedication and commitment, we can achieve a liberated mind and lasting well-being.

The journey to a calmer mind

Following our journey towards a calmer mind, let us now see which paths can lead us to inner peace. Each of these paths can bring us closer and closer to our longed-for peace of mind; let's see what they are about and how they benefit us.

Cultivate self-compassion. In our eagerness to improve, we are often too hard on ourselves. Let's learn to treat ourselves with kindness and understanding, recognizing that we all make mistakes and that it's okay not to be perfect.

Allow yourself to be human and forgive yourself for your failures. Self-compassion gives us the strength and peace we need to overcome challenges and grow on our path to peace of mind.

Free ourselves from comparison. Constant comparison with others can lead to excessive and unbalanced thinking. Remember that each person has his or her own path and that we are all unique.

Instead of comparing yourself to others, focus on your own growth and development. Celebrate your accomplishments and recognize your own strengths. In doing so, you will build solid self-esteem and find satisfaction in your own progress.

Practice gratitude. Gratitude is a powerful tool that helps us change our perspective and find joy in the little things in life.

Cultivate the habit of being grateful for what you have, for the people around you and for the experiences that have shaped you. By focusing on the positive, you will decrease overthinking and create a more harmonious and comforting mental environment.

Connecting with nature. Nature provides us with an endless source of peace and tranquility. Take time to be outdoors, breathe in the fresh air and connect with the natural environment.

Observe the beauty that surrounds you, listen to the sounds of nature and allow its serenity to envelop you. This connection with nature will help you clear your mind and find balance amidst the hustle and bustle of everyday life.

Nurturing emotional well-being. Taking care of our emotional health is essential to maintaining a calm mind. Allow yourself to express your emotions in a healthy way, whether through writing, music, art or talking to someone you trust.

In addition, seek out activities that bring you joy and satisfaction, such as pursuing a hobby or spending time with loved ones. By prioritizing your emotional well-being, you will strengthen your resilience against overthinking.

Learning to let go of control. Sometimes, overthinking arises from our eagerness to control every aspect of our lives.

Accept that there are things beyond our control and that it is okay to let circumstances take their natural course. Trust yourself and the process of life. By letting go of control, you will find greater calmness and fluidity in your thoughts.

This journey to a calmer mind is full of opportunities for growth and self-transformation. Every small step counts and we deserve to experience calm and inner peace.

The power of the present

The power of the present refers to the ability to live fully in the present moment and take advantage of all the opportunities and experiences it offers us.

It consists of being aware and present in the here and now, instead of being stuck in the past or worrying about the future.

When we focus on the present, we can experience a sense of calmness and mental clarity. It allows us to enjoy the little things in life and be more connected to ourselves and our surroundings.

By being present, we are able to appreciate and savor each moment without letting thoughts and worries distract us. The power of the present also helps us make more informed and conscious decisions.

By being fully present in our interactions and activities, we can pay attention to the details and cues offered by the environment. This allows us to make better decisions that are aligned with our needs and values.

In addition, living in the present frees us from the burden of the past and anxiety about the future. It helps us to let go of past worries and regrets, as well as future expectations and fears.

It allows us to focus on what we can control in the present moment and accept what we cannot change. Practicing the power of the present requires training and discipline.

Did you know that practicing certain techniques can help us develop this ability to live in the present? By exercising the power of the present, we can experience greater satisfaction and fulfillment in our lives.

It helps us to free ourselves from stress, anxiety and mental exhaustion caused by constantly living in the past or in the future. It allows us to enjoy each moment and be more connected with ourselves and others.

Among the techniques that can help us are the practice of *mindfulness*, meditation, conscious breathing and focusing on our senses and present sensations.

A recent study found that strategies such as meditation and mindfulness can decrease symptoms of stress, anxiety and recurrent thoughts by 50%.

Let me tell you the story of Lucia, who struggled for a long time with obsessive thoughts. She began meditating and working with a therapist to change her destructive thought patterns.

At first, he did not notice much improvement, but his obsessive thoughts diminished noticeably after months of constant practice.

Although it is normal for these thoughts to return at times, you will learn to deal with them more effectively over time.

It is important to remember that there are no quick and easy solutions to overcoming excessive thinking. It is necessary to commit to a long-term strategy that includes techniques for controlling thoughts, identifying triggers, and developing coping skills.

Cognitive-behavioral therapy is one of the most effective tools in this regard, as it has proven to be as effective as medication in treating depression. These are powerful tools that can make a difference in your life.

Therapy, meditation and mindfulness are all beneficial practices for maintaining long-term concentration. All have been shown to reduce anxiety and despair, and help train attention and concentration.

Don't forget that taking care of your physical health is also critical to maintaining long-term concentration. Regular exercise has been shown to reduce worry and tension and improve mood.

The power of the present lies in maintaining long-term attention and avoiding overthinking. It is not necessary to control all your thoughts.

Accept that they are transient and don't judge them. With practice and dedication, you will be able to maintain long-term attention and avoid excess. Don't get discouraged and stay consistent.

To live in the present, the here and now, I want to give you a list of actions that have served me throughout my life, and have been of great value to keep my mind away from repetitive thoughts, control my mind and the multiple episodes of stress that I have suffered; I hope they are to your liking and of valuable help.

Living in the present can be transformative for our lives. There are several aspects that will help us make the most of the power of the present.

From maintaining a positive, growth-oriented attitude to learning to say "no," each topic provides practical tools for enjoying a full and productive life.

Maintain a cheerful, growth-oriented attitude and a positive mindset: A positive attitude and a growth-oriented mindset allow us to face challenges with optimism and learn from every experience. Cultivating this attitude positively influences our overall well-being.

Learning to say "no": Saying "no" in an assertive way is fundamental to establish limits and prioritize our needs. Setting healthy boundaries and knowing how to communicate them in a respectful manner is of utmost importance.

Mastering the ability to concentrate and self-control by avoiding overthinking situations: Overthinking can distract us and limit our focus on the present. There are several practical strategies that allow us to master concentration and self-control, allowing us to be very present in each moment.

Maintain concentration by avoiding excessive thinking: Concentration on a task is essential to achieve satisfactory results; we must always be aware of the appearance of intrusive thoughts to avoid them and improve our ability to concentrate on the tasks we perform.

Long-term strategy to reduce necessary musings: Necessary musings can drain our energy and hinder our personal growth. In any case, it is advisable to create a long-term strategy to reduce these cavilings and focus on what really matters.

Avoid speculating about what will happen in the future: Excessive speculation about the future can generate anxiety and distract us from the present. Let's avoid this speculation and learn to trust our personal process.

Avoid distractions: Constant distractions can hinder our focus on the present. Avoid distractions and let's stay focused on our daily activities.

Develop a daily schedule that includes set times for each activity and responsibility: A well-structured schedule provides us with a framework to organize our activities efficiently. We will learn how to develop a daily schedule that allows us to prioritize our responsibilities and find the right balance.

Have a list of tasks and prioritize the most important ones: Effectively managing our tasks helps us avoid procrastination and maximize our productivity. Practicing techniques to create to-do lists and prioritizing the most important tasks will allow us to move towards our goals more effectively.

Turn off all electronic devices: Technology can be a constant distraction in our lives. Let's unplug our electronic devices at certain times and begin to enjoy moments of peace and quiet.

Set goals to maintain motivation and ensure we meet our objectives: Setting clear and achievable goals gives us direction and drives us forward.

In order to achieve our objectives, we need to stay focused on them: Sustained concentration on our goals allows us to move forward steadily. Let's keep our attention and energy focused on achieving our goals.

Make plans for activities that will bring us joy during our free time: Free time is a valuable moment to recharge energies and enjoy activities that will bring us happiness; let's make plans for pleasurable activities and make the most of these moments.

Take regular breaks: This is essential to maintain our energy and productivity; taking advantage of them effectively will help us maintain a healthy balance.

Make an effort to relax before starting work: Pre-work relaxation helps us to prepare mentally and emotionally for the tasks ahead, so we incorporate relaxation techniques into our daily routine.

Try to keep the mind active: An active and agile mind allows us to face challenges and learn continuously.

Let's surround ourselves with optimistic and encouraging people: Our social environment influences our well-being and attitude. It is very important to surround ourselves with optimistic and encouraging people as they will support us in our personal growth.

Maintain healthy relationships and a network of helpful people: Healthy relationships and a network of helpful contacts can open up opportunities and provide emotional support.

If we experience symptoms of anxiety, sadness or stress, seek the help of a trained expert: It is essential to take care of our mental and emotional health. Seek professional help if we have persistent symptoms of anxiety, sadness or stress.

Dedicate time to disconnect and recharge our batteries: In an increasingly fast-paced world, it is essential to dedicate time to disconnect and recharge our energies. This time of rest is very valuable, and it is vital to incorporate it into our daily routine to maintain a healthy balance.

Living in the present allows us to experience greater satisfaction and make the most of each moment. These practical strategies will help us cultivate a full and productive life focused on the power of the present.

CHAPTER 6

Overthinking and its impact

Overthinking is a pattern of thinking characterized by constant rumination, obsession and exaggerated worry about past, present or future situations.

It is a repetitive and negative mental activity that consumes a great amount of energy and attention, impairing our quality of life and emotional well-being.

The impact of overthinking can be significant and encompass different areas of our lives. On an emotional level, it can generate anxiety, stress, frustration and irritability.

Our mind is trapped in a cycle of negative and catastrophic thoughts, which affects our self-esteem and self-confidence.

In addition, overthinking can interfere with our ability to concentrate and make clear decisions. It distracts us from our tasks and prevents us from enjoying the present.

It can also have repercussions on our relationships, as we become so immersed in our thoughts that we become less present and attentive to others.

On the physical level, prolonged overthinking can manifest itself in symptoms such as headaches, muscle tension, sleep disorders and even more serious health problems such as gastrointestinal or cardiovascular disorders.

Chronic stress associated with overthinking can weaken our immune system and have a negative impact on our overall health.

It is important to be aware of the negative impact of overthinking in order to address it and find effective strategies to manage it.

By learning to recognize when our thoughts become excessive, we can take steps to control them and redirect them to more positive and constructive topics.

The first step in counteracting the impact of overthinking is to cultivate awareness and mindfulness.

Learning to observe our thoughts without judging them and without completely identifying with them allows us to distance ourselves and gain perspective.

This helps us to question the validity and veracity of our negative thoughts, and to find healthier ways of dealing with the situations that concern us.

Other useful strategies include practicing relaxation techniques, such as deep breathing, meditation and regular physical exercise. These activities help us to release accumulated tension in our body and calm our minds.

It is also important to cultivate a mindset of gratitude and appreciation for the positive things in our lives. Focusing on what is good and what we can control helps us to counteract negative thought patterns and generate a more balanced perspective.

Overthinking has a significant impact on our emotional, mental and physical lives. Recognizing this impact is the first step in addressing it and finding effective strategies to manage it.

Through mindfulness, attention to our thoughts and the adoption of healthy habits, we can free ourselves from excessive thinking and live a more balanced and satisfying life.

Excessive thoughts and stress

In our daily lives, we often find ourselves caught in a spiral of negative thoughts and worries that seem to have no end.

These excessive thoughts can become exhausting and, over time, contribute to the development of chronic stress that affects our mental and physical health.

There is a deep connection between excessive thoughts and chronic stress, understanding how they feed on chemicals and discovering strategies to free ourselves from their paralyzing embrace.

The vicious circle between excessive thoughts and chronic stress: Excessive thoughts and chronic stress are closely related and can form a vicious circle that is difficult to break.

When we find ourselves trapped in a wheel of negative thoughts and constant worries, our body and mind react as if we are in constant danger.

This triggers the stress response, which activates a cascade of chemical reactions in our body, including the release of stress hormones such as cortisol and adrenaline.

In turn, prolonged chronic stress has a negative impact on our ability to handle excessive thoughts.

Our nervous system becomes overloaded, making it difficult for us to find calm and perspective in the face of the worries that beset us.

Chronic stress can also affect our quality of sleep, eating and ability to relax, which increases the intensity of excessive thoughts and perpetuates the stress cycle.

Chronic stress has significant consequences for our health, both mentally and physically. On the mental side, it can contribute to the development of anxiety disorders, depression and concentration problems.

Mental and emotional fatigue becomes a constant burden, and our abilities to solve problems and make effective decisions are compromised.

On a physical level, chronic stress can weaken our immune system, increasing susceptibility to disease and infection.

It can also trigger headaches, digestive problems, muscle tension and cardiovascular problems.

In addition, prolonged chronic stress can accelerate cellular aging and increase the risk of chronic diseases such as diabetes, hypertension and heart disease.

Excessive thoughts and stress are specifically related and can affect different aspects of our lives.

Below, I want to show you what this relationship looks like and include some examples so that you can understand it more easily:

Physical and emotional health: Excessive thoughts can have a significant impact on our physical and emotional health, as they are linked to chronic stress. Prolonged stress can trigger a fight or flight response in our body, which can lead to physical symptoms such as headaches, muscle tension, digestive problems and weakened immune systems.

Imagine you are going through a stressful work situation and find yourself constantly worrying about your performance and fearful of making mistakes. These excessive thoughts and the resulting stress can manifest themselves in frequent headaches and stomach problems, affecting your physical well-being.

Interpersonal relationships: Excessive thoughts can affect our interpersonal relationships, as they can make us more irritable, anxious and emotionally drained. The stress associated with excessive thoughts can hinder effective communication and generate conflicts in our relationships.

If you are constantly worried about the opinions of others and fear being judged, you may avoid participating in social activities or expressing your opinions. This can lead to a lack of connection with others and negatively affect your relationships.

Productivity and performance: Excessive thoughts can affect our ability to concentrate and perform tasks efficiently, which can decrease our productivity and performance at work or in other areas of life. Stress associated with excessive thoughts can make it difficult to make decisions and take action.

If you find yourself constantly worrying about the future and ruminating about possible negative scenarios, you are likely to have difficulty concentrating on your work. This can lead to a decrease in your productivity and work performance, and even more stress.

Self-esteem and confidence: Excessive negative thoughts can undermine our self-esteem and self-confidence. When we focus on self-critical thoughts and constantly doubt our abilities, it is more difficult to have a positive self-image and confidence in our abilities.

If you have excessive thoughts about not being good enough at your job, you may begin to question your skills and value as a professional. This can affect your self-esteem and make you feel insecure in the work environment.

Overall well-being: Excessive thoughts and chronic stress can affect our overall well-being, both physically and emotionally. They can generate a sense of exhaustion, overwhelm and constant emotional drain, which negatively impacts our overall quality of life.

If you are constantly preoccupied with multiple aspects of your life, such as work, personal relationships and family responsibilities, you may experience an overwhelming sense of stress and exhaustion. This can

decrease your enjoyment of daily activities and affect your overall well-being.

Sleep and rest: Excessive thoughts can make it difficult to sleep and get adequate rest. When our mind is filled with worries and recurring thoughts, it can be difficult to fall asleep or stay asleep during the night. Stress associated with excessive thoughts can lead to insomnia or poor quality sleep.

If you find yourself constantly reviewing past situations or worrying about the future while trying to sleep, you are likely to have difficulty falling asleep. This can lead to fatigue and affect your energy and mental clarity during the day.

Decision making: Excessive thoughts can make it difficult to make decisions, as we find ourselves trapped in a cycle of over-analysis and fear of making mistakes. The stress associated with excessive thoughts can lead to indecision and difficulty in making important decisions in different areas of our lives.

If you are frequently worried about making the wrong career decision, you may spend a lot of time analyzing all possible options and fearing negative consequences. This can lead to procrastination and missing important opportunities for growth and development.

Emotional self-control: Excessive thoughts can make emotional self-control more difficult, as we become more susceptible to intense emotional reactions. The stress associated with excessive thoughts can make us feel overwhelmed by emotions such as anxiety, anger or sadness, and we find it more difficult to regulate our emotional responses.

If you find yourself constantly worrying about things that could go wrong in your life, you may experience episodes of intense anxiety that you find difficult to control. This can affect your interpersonal relationships and your overall emotional well-being.

Self-demanding: Excessive thoughts can lead to excessive self-demanding, where we set really high expectations and constantly push ourselves to achieve perfection. The stress associated with excessive thinking can lead to a sense of constant dissatisfaction and a feeling of never being good enough.

If you find yourself constantly thinking about all the things you could have done better and feeling dissatisfied even when you achieve important goals, you may be experiencing excessive self-demand. This can lead to chronic stress and negatively affect your self-esteem.

Creativity and mental fluidity: Excessive thoughts can block our creativity and mental fluidity, as we find ourselves trapped in rigid thought patterns and constant suspicion. The stress associated with overthinking can make it difficult to generate new ideas and limit our ability to solve problems in innovative ways.

If you find yourself constantly worrying about making mistakes in your creative work, you may become blocked and find it difficult to generate new ideas. This can affect your professional performance and your ability to excel in your field.

Remember that each person may experience these aspects uniquely and in different areas of their lives. If you identify with any of them and feel that excessive thoughts and stress are negatively diminishing your well-being, it is advisable to seek professional support to learn stress management techniques and cultivate a calmer, more balanced mind.

Breaking the cycle of excessive thoughts and chronic stress: Convenient, effective strategies exist to break the cycle of excessive thoughts and chronic stress, and thus regain our peace of mind and overall well-being.

Awareness and self-observation: The first step is to become aware of our excessive thoughts and how it happens to us.

Observing our thought patterns allows us to identify recurring needs and understand how they relate to our chronic stress.

Relaxation techniques: Practicing relaxation techniques, such as deep breathing, meditation and yoga, can help us reduce stress activation and calm our minds.

These practices promote relaxation and allow us to cultivate a calmer and more balanced attitude towards life's challenges.

Cognitive restructuring: Learning to challenge and replace our negative thoughts with more realistic and positive thoughts can make a big difference in our well-being.

Identifying the cognitive biases that distort our thinking helps us to question their validity and adopt a more objective perspective.

Time management and limit setting: Organizing our tasks and priorities effectively helps us reduce the feeling of being overwhelmed.

Setting healthy limits on our responsibilities and learning to say "no" when necessary allows us to spend time taking care of ourselves and getting adequate rest.

Social and professional support: Seeking support from family, friends and mental health professionals can be invaluable in the process of overcoming excessive thoughts and chronic stress.

Sharing our concerns and seeking guidance provides us with different perspectives and additional tools to address these challenges.

The connection between excessive thoughts and chronic stress is profound and can have a significant impact on our quality of life. However, we can free ourselves from its paralyzing embrace by understanding this relationship and applying effective strategies.

These examples are only representative and each person may experience the effects of excessive thoughts and stress in unique ways.

If you identify with any of these aspects and are dealing with excessive thoughts that are negatively worsening your life, it is important to consider seeking professional help to learn stress management strategies and foster a calmer, more balanced mind.

If you would like to learn more about stress and discover more strategies to manage it effectively, I invite you to consult my book "Inner Serenity: Discover the Path to Balance and Tranquility".

Explore these valuable resources and begin your journey to a calmer, healthier life.

When to seek professional help?

Excessive thoughts can be an emotional and mental burden for those who experience them. We all have recurring thoughts at some point, but when they become overwhelming, persistent and negatively detract from our quality of life, it is important to recognize if they are getting out of control.

But how do we identify if our excessive thoughts are becoming problematic? When is the right time to seek help from a mental health specialist?

Some signs that our excessive thoughts are getting out of control are:

Interference with daily activities: If your excessive thoughts begin to interfere with your daily activities, such as work, relationships, or enjoyment of pleasurable activities, it is an indication that they are getting out of control. For example, if you find it difficult to concentrate on a task because of constant intrusive thoughts.

Increased anxiety and stress: If your excessive thoughts cause a significant level of anxiety and stress to the point of affecting your emotional and physical well-being, it is a sign that you need specialized care. Constant worrying and ruminating can trigger anxiety symptoms, such as rapid heartbeat, excessive sweating and shortness of breath.

Negative thought patterns: If your excessive thoughts follow negative patterns, such as always anticipating the worst or focusing on the negative, it may indicate that you are trapped in a destructive cycle of thoughts. These patterns can negatively influence your outlook on life and your overall mood.

Loss of sleep and exhaustion: If your excessive thoughts prevent you from falling asleep or wake you up during the night, causing a lack of adequate rest, it is a clear sign that you need help. Lack of adequate sleep can worsen anxiety and affect your overall health.

Some signs that we need to seek the help of a specialist to control our excessive thoughts:

Persistence of excessive thoughts: If your excessive thoughts persist for an extended period of time, despite your efforts to control them, it is advisable to seek professional help. A mental health specialist can help you understand the underlying causes of your thoughts and provide you with effective strategies to manage them.

Significant impact on your life: If your excessive thoughts are negatively impacting your personal, work or social life, and you are unable to function properly because of them, it's time to seek help. A specialist can help you identify problem areas and work with you to develop healthier coping skills.

Impaired mental and emotional health: If your excessive thoughts are causing a deterioration in your mental and emotional health, such as depression, panic attacks or other anxiety disorders, it is essential to seek the help of a specialist. They can provide you with a proper diagnosis and recommend appropriate treatment.

Failed attempts at self-management: If you have tried to manage your excessive thoughts on your own, using techniques such as meditation or writing, but have not experienced significant improvements, it is time to consider professional help. A specialist can assess your situation more fully and offer you therapeutic approaches tailored to your specific needs.

Recognizing if your excessive thoughts are getting out of control is an important step toward self-care and mental wellness.

If you experience signs that your excessive thoughts are negatively worsening your daily life, such as interfering with your activities, increasing anxiety and stress, or maintaining negative thought patterns, it is essential to consider the help of a mental health specialist.

Remember that seeking support is not a sign of weakness, but a sign of courage and a desire to improve your quality of life.

In my book "Inner Serenity: Discover the Path to Balance and Tranquility" in this self-help collection, you will find additional information and practical strategies to address these challenges and find the calmness of mind you so desire.

Conclusion

By freeing our minds from the cycle of excessive thinking, we open ourselves to a life full of calm, peace and serenity.

We free ourselves from the chains of constant worry and allow ourselves to experience joy and fulfillment in the present.

As we move away from limiting thoughts and connect with our inner self, we find a greater sense of clarity and purpose in our lives.

In the journey of exploring and freeing our mind from the cycle of overthinking, we have traveled a road full of learnings and discoveries about our emotional well-being.

Throughout this ebook entitled "Free Your Mind: Break the Cycle of Overthinking," we have explored the causes, effects and strategies for managing and overcoming excessive thoughts that lead to stress and lower our mental health.

We have learned that excessive thoughts are a common phenomenon, but we can also identify them as a barrier that prevents us from living fully and enjoying the present.

It has become clear the various ways in which excessive thoughts can manifest in our mind, from ruminating on past situations to worrying excessively about the future. These thought patterns take us away from mental calm and plunge us into a state of chronic stress.

During this journey, I have had the privilege of sharing with you the tools and practical tips that can make a difference in your daily life.

We have also explored a wide range of strategies and techniques to break the cycle of overthinking and free our minds from its tyranny.

We have discovered the importance of mindfulness and meditation, which help us cultivate focused attention and free us from constant rumination.

We learned about the practice of self-compassion and acceptance, which allow us to embrace our thoughts without judgment and find a more compassionate perspective towards ourselves.

In addition, we have explored how the regular practice of relaxation techniques and physical exercise can help us to release accumulated tension in our body and mind, bringing us greater balance and serenity.

The importance of setting healthy boundaries and practicing self-care has also been emphasized, reminding us to set aside time for ourselves and prioritize our mental health.

Understanding and controlling excessive thoughts is an ongoing and constantly evolving process. Therefore, I would like to invite you to continue exploring more self-help and personal development texts, which can provide you with even more support and knowledge on your path to serenity and emotional balance.

In particular, I would like to recommend you my book "Inner Serenity: Discover the Path to Balance and Tranquility", which is part of the collection I have written with the objective of helping you in your journey towards a more fulfilling and satisfying life.

This book focuses specifically on stress and provides a comprehensive guide to understanding its causes, identifying its effects on your well-being and most importantly, discovering practical strategies to cultivate inner serenity and emotional balance.

Through "Inner Serenity", you will learn effective techniques to manage stress, develop emotional resilience and find tranquility in the midst of daily chaos.

You will explore different approaches, such as meditation, mindfulness and self-care, that will help you find your own inner peace and build a solid foundation for your mental and emotional well-being.

Remember that the path to inner serenity is not linear or static. It requires dedication, practice and a constant commitment to yourself. However, each small step you take on this journey will bring you closer and closer to the full and balanced life you desire.

Remember that transformation begins from within, and by committing to the process of liberation, you will be taking an important step towards a more balanced, conscious and fulfilled life.

Thank you for joining me on this journey of mental liberation. I wish you success and fulfillment on your path to inner serenity, keep exploring and discovering your true potential!

With love,
Simone Keys

BONUS 1

Visualization and personal transformation

Visualization can be an effective way to explore and delve deeper within ourselves. It is a powerful tool that allows us to access our imagination and create vivid and meaningful mental images.

Through visualization, we can connect with our deepest goals, dreams and desires, and use this powerful tool to enhance our self-knowledge and personal growth.

In this bonus, we will learn some visualization exercises that will help us transform our lives in a positive and meaningful way.

Let's look at some visualization exercises that can help us enhance our self-knowledge:

The hall of mirrors: Imagine you walk into a room full of mirrors. Each one reflects a different facet of your personality, your strengths, your weaknesses, your dreams and your fears. Look closely at each reflection and reflect on what it reveals about you. Use this visualization to gain a deeper understanding of who you are.

The inner garden: Close your eyes and imagine that you are walking through a beautiful garden. Each element of the garden represents an aspect of your life: the flowers symbolize your relationships, the trees represent your personal growth, and the water reflects your inner tranquility. Notice how each element looks and how they interact with each other. Reflect on what you would like to change, improve or cultivate in your inner garden. Use this visualization to explore your desires and goals in different areas of your life.

Our imagination has a powerful impact on our perception and our ability to create positive change in our lives. Let's use imagination as a tool for positive change.

Travel to the future: Close your eyes and imagine that you are in a distant future, where you have achieved all your goals and feel fully realized. Observe your life in this future and visualize all the details: how you feel, what you have achieved, how you relate to others, etc. Use this visualization to connect with your vision of success and to set clear and motivating goals in the present.

Transformation of limiting beliefs: Identify a belief that is holding you back from moving toward your goals. Close your eyes and imagine holding that belief in your hands. Visualize transforming that belief into something positive and empowering. Imagine the belief becoming a seed that you plant in the fertile soil of your mind, and enjoy how it grows into a new belief that strengthens you and propels you toward success.

Remember that visualization is a personal and unique practice for each person. You can adapt the visualization exercises to your own needs and preferences. Find a quiet place, close your eyes, breathe deeply and immerse yourself in the imaginative experience.

By using these powerful visualizations, you will develop a deeper connection with yourself, discovering new possibilities and potentialities in your life.

Visualization not only helps you focus on your goals and dreams, but also provides you with an effective tool to overcome obstacles, strengthen your confidence and awaken your creativity.

As you immerse yourself in your imagination, you open yourself to new perspectives and possibilities, creating a solid foundation for growth and positive change in your life. In this way, you can move toward manifesting your true self and living a full and meaningful life.

Visualizations are a valuable tool for personal transformation, allowing you to enhance your self-knowledge, explore your desires and goals, and transform limiting beliefs into empowering ones.

BONUS 2

Affirmations for self-transformation

Affirmations are positive statements that help us to reprogram our minds and promote positive change in our lives. In the context of the Enneagram, we can use specific affirmations based on each personality type to promote self-transformation and personal growth.

Next, let's see which affirmations are effective in helping each personality type on a daily basis:

Personality Type 1 - The Perfectionist

- I am enough as I am. I allow myself to make mistakes and learn from them.
- I recognize that progress is more important than perfection. I allow myself to grow and evolve instead of seeking absolute excellence.
- I appreciate my accomplishments and recognize that success is not determined solely by the end results, but by the effort and dedication I put into each task.

Personality Type 2 - The Helper

- I value my own well-being and set healthy boundaries. I allow myself to be supported and cared for.
- I learn to say "no" when necessary and set healthy boundaries to maintain my emotional and physical well-being.

- I recognize that taking care of myself allows me to be in a better position to help others in a more effective and sustainable way.

Personality Type 3 - The Achiever

- My value does not depend on my external achievements. My authenticity is my greatest strength.
- My worth is not only linked to my external achievements, but to my authenticity and the quality of my personal relationships.
- I appreciate the moments of rest and enjoyment, recognizing that true happiness depends not only on achieving goals, but also on enjoying the journey.

Personality Type 4 - The Individualist

- I celebrate my uniqueness and accept myself in all my facets. My creativity illuminates my path.
- I explore and embrace my inner diversity. Each part of me has its purpose and contributes to my uniqueness and personal growth.
- I appreciate the power of my creativity and allow it to guide my choices, bringing new perspectives and opportunities into my life.

Personality Type 5 - The Researcher

- I trust my inner wisdom and share my knowledge with others. I am part of the whole.

- I trust my intuition and inner wisdom when making decisions and seeking knowledge. My unique perspective enriches my environment and benefits others.
- I generously share my knowledge and experiences, knowing that in doing so, I contribute to the growth and development of those around me.

Personality Type 6 - The Loyal

- I trust myself and the process of life. I am brave and capable of facing any challenge.
- I am confident in myself and in my ability to face challenges. I am constantly growing and developing, and I have the courage to overcome any obstacle that comes my way.
- I cultivate relationships based on loyalty and mutual trust, creating a supportive and collaborative environment in my life.

Personality Type 7 - The Enthusiast

- I find fulfillment in the present and appreciate the blessings of each moment. Joy is within me.
- I find joy and fulfillment in every present moment, appreciating the little things that bring me happiness and gratitude.
- I cultivate a mindset of abundance and optimism, recognizing that joy and happiness are internal states that I can nurture and experience at any time.

Personality Type 8 - The Protector

- I am strong and powerful, I allow myself to be vulnerable and show compassion to others.
- I recognize my personal strength and power, and also allow myself to show vulnerability and compassion to others.
- I use my strength and protection to care for and support those I care about, creating a safe and loving environment around me.

Personality Type 9 - Peacemaker

- I assert myself and express my needs clearly and assertively. My voice is important and valued.
- I assert and express my needs and desires in a clear and respectful manner, knowing that my voice and opinions are important and valued.
- I seek harmony and peaceful conflict resolution, creating a space where everyone feels heard and understood.

For the good use of these and other positive affirmations, it is recommended:

Be aware of your thoughts: Observe your thoughts and detect negative or limiting patterns. Identify the beliefs you want to change and replace them with positive affirmations.

Choose powerful affirmations: Create affirmations that resonate with you and are relevant to your personal growth. They should be positive, in the present tense and formulated in the first person.

Repeat and reinforce: Repeat your affirmations daily, preferably in moments of peace, when waking up or before going to sleep. Reinforce their effectiveness by visualizing yourself living the reality you desire while reciting them.

Reinforce your affirmations with consistent actions: Affirmations are most effective when they are accompanied by consistent actions. Align your actions and behaviors with the beliefs and attitudes you wish to manifest in your life.

By using affirmations based on each personality type of the Enneagram, you can direct your focus to the specific aspects you wish to strengthen and transform in your life.

Remember that affirmations are not a magical solution but a tool to help you reprogram your mind and create positive change in your life.

Using effective affirmations requires commitment and consistent practice. As you practice and commit to affirmations, you will gradually begin to cultivate a more positive, confident and empowered mindset.

Change takes time and effort. Be patient with yourself and maintain an attitude of openness and receptivity. Do not expect instant results, but practice consistently and trust the process.

By adopting positive and realistic affirmations, you can reprogram your mind and begin to align your thoughts, beliefs and actions with your true potential.

Don't be discouraged if at first you don't feel an immediate change, consistent practice and perseverance are key to lasting results. Over time, affirmations can help you change your negative thought patterns, strengthen your self-confidence and enable you to achieve your goals and aspirations.

Adapt affirmations to your own language and way of thinking. Choose words and phrases that generate a sense of connection and empowerment. Affirmations must be realistic and believable to you, as your mind needs to accept them as true to be effective.

As you practice affirmations consistently and integrate them into your daily life, you will begin to notice positive changes in the way you think, feel and act. For example, if you affirm that you are a healthy person, support that affirmation with healthy food choices and regular exercise.

Powerful affirmations can be an invaluable tool for self-transformation and personal growth. By combining effective affirmations with clear visualizations and consistent actions, you can cultivate a positive mindset and build a life more aligned with your true self.

BONUS 3

Cultivating Emotional Resilience

Emotional resilience is an essential ability to face life's challenges and adversities with strength and adaptability. It allows us to recover from difficulties and maintain a positive attitude.

Emotional resilience is essential to our emotional and mental well-being, helping us to cope with stressful situations, overcome failures and maintain a positive mindset. By cultivating it, we develop the ability to manage our emotions in a healthy way and build a solid foundation for personal growth.

There are several aspects that emotional resilience can strengthen in our personality. For example:

Adaptation to change: Allows us to adapt to life's changes and transitions more effectively. It helps us to accept and overcome obstacles, finding new opportunities in the midst of adversity.

Stress management: Helps us to manage stress more efficiently. It allows us to identify our emotional responses to stressful situations and take measures to reduce the negative impact of stress on our health and well-being.

Self-confidence: Strengthens our self-confidence. It helps us believe in our abilities to overcome challenges and gives us the courage to face difficult situations.

There are several practices that can help you strengthen your emotional resilience. Here are some recommended exercises and techniques:

Emotional self-awareness: Take the time to explore and understand your own emotions. Practice mindfulness and introspection to recognize your emotional patterns and how they affect you. This will allow you to develop a greater awareness of yourself and your emotional responses.

Building a support network: Cultivate strong and supportive relationships with family, friends and members of your community. Share your feelings and experiences with people you trust, as this can give you the emotional support you need during difficult times.

Seek social support: Seek support from people close to you, such as friends, family or support groups. Sharing your experiences and emotions with others can help you gain different perspectives and feel understood. Participate in social activities that provide positive connections and allow you to feel part of a community.

Practice self-compassion: Learn to treat yourself with kindness and understanding when you face challenges or make mistakes. Recognize that we all make mistakes and that personal growth involves learning from them. Instead of judging yourself harshly, practice self-compassion and give yourself permission to be human.

Maintain a learning attitude: Cultivate a mindset that is open and receptive to continuous learning. Consider every experience as an opportunity to grow and learn more about yourself. Be curious and willing to explore new perspectives and approaches in life.

Acceptance and adaptation: Learn to accept circumstances that you cannot change and focus on adapting to them. Recognize that change is an inevitable part of life and look for new ways to deal with challenges.

Problem-solving practice: Develops effective problem-solving skills. Break challenges into smaller, more manageable steps and look for creative solutions. This will help you face obstacles with a proactive mindset.

Self-care: Prioritize your physical and mental well-being. Spending time on activities that bring you joy, rest and rejuvenation is critical to cultivating emotional resilience. Set healthy boundaries in your life and learn to say "no" when necessary. Self-care also involves eating a balanced diet, getting enough rest and maintaining a proper sleep routine.

Develop coping skills: Learn healthy coping techniques to manage stress and negative emotions. This may include regular physical exercise, relaxation techniques such as meditation or deep breathing, and finding activities that help you express your emotions, such as writing in a journal or practicing a hobby.

Cultivate positive thoughts: Practice gratitude and focus on positive aspects of your life. Challenge your negative thoughts and replace them with positive affirmations. Make a list of past accomplishments and personal strengths to remind you of your ability to overcome obstacles and face challenges.

Developing emotional resilience is an ongoing process that requires practice and dedication. By strengthening our ability to manage emotions and adapt to difficult situations, we can face life's challenges with confidence and maintain a positive outlook.

Use these exercises and techniques to build a solid foundation for your emotional well-being and personal growth.

Remember to be kind to yourself during this journey of self-transformation.

BONUS 4

Building Healthy Relationships

Healthy, meaningful relationships are fundamental to our emotional and personal well-being. They provide us with support, companionship and a sense of deep connection. However, building healthy relationships can be challenging, as each individual brings unique experiences and patterns of behavior.

The basis of any healthy relationship is open and honest communication; this implies:

- Learn to express our feelings, thoughts and needs in a clear and respectful manner.
- Actively listen to your partner, friend or family member, showing genuine interest and empathy.
- Establishing clear boundaries in relationships is essential to ensure mutual respect and emotional balance.
- Learn to say "no" when necessary and to set limits in uncomfortable situations.

Trust is a fundamental pillar of healthy relationships. To build it, it is important:

- Be authentic.
- Fulfill promises and commitments.
- Avoid manipulation, dishonesty and deception.

- Practice empathy and understanding by putting yourself in the other person's shoes and validating their emotions and perspectives.
- Identify and address toxic patterns, abusive behaviors or disrespect in relationships.

Overcoming toxic patterns requires personal work and a commitment to each other. You can seek professional support or consider therapy to work on healing and change.

It is important to remember that each relationship is unique and requires constant attention. By developing a greater awareness of yourself and your relationship patterns, you will be able to nurture and strengthen your connections with others.

Remember that healthy relationships also involve taking care of yourself. Set boundaries and make time for physical and mental self-care.

By building healthy relationships, you will be cultivating an environment of support, trust and mutual growth. Through mindfulness and commitment, you can create lasting, meaningful relationships that propel you toward a fuller, more satisfying life.

Thank you for your interest in reading my work

I hope you have found this book interesting and that by reading my experiences, you have gained ideas and inspiration to help you on your own path to self-improvement, mental health and happiness.

I invite you to continue on the path of self-help.

Keep reading the entire collection of self-help books I have created for you, keep getting ideas and inspiration for self-improvement, mental health and happiness.

Your help means a lot

If you liked this book, one of the best things you could do for me would be to leave a review on the website where you bought it. It won't take you long, but it would be great if you could spare those minutes for me.

If you give my work a high rating, more people will see it and, in turn, it will improve their lives, health and happiness.

May your journey be filled with peace and abundance,
Simone Keys

www.ingramcontent.com/pod-product-compliance
Lightning Source LLC
Chambersburg PA
CBHW050251010526
44107CB00003B/269